T0322005

unprocessed
made easy

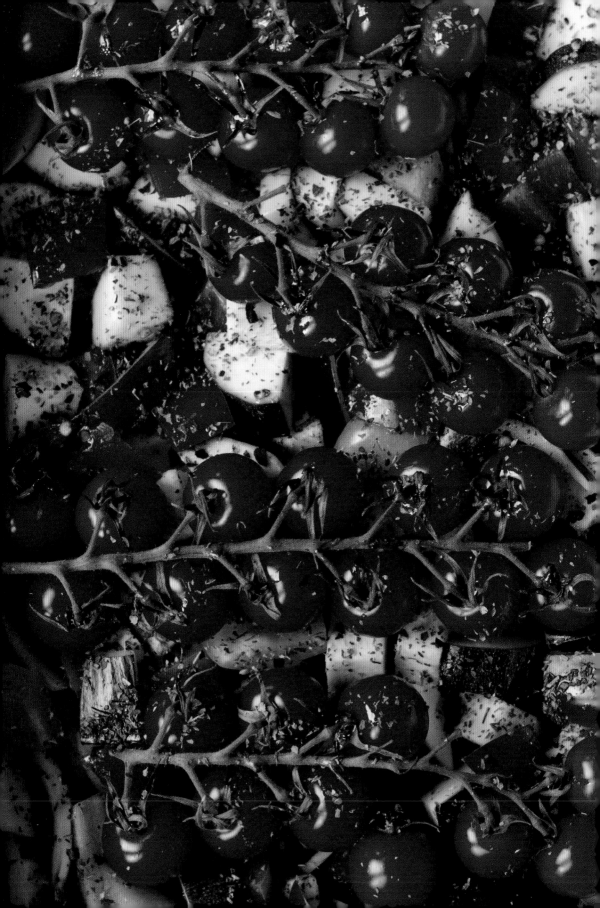

unprocessed
made easy

Quick, Healthy, Family-Friendly Meals

DELICIA BALE ANutr

POP PRESS

Contents

Reduce
ultra-processed
foods in your diet
in a simple and
delicious way

Introduction

Everyone seems to be worried about eating too much ultra-processed food — or UPF. These foods are convenient and often delicious, but overconsuming them has been found to have many negative health implications. *Unprocessed Made Easy* is your simple guide to reducing the amount of UPF in your diet with straightforward recipes and simple swaps!

What are UPFs?

UPFs are industrially produced foods that contain ingredients that are not typically used in a home kitchen, such as preservatives, emulsifiers, sweeteners, artificial colours and flavours used to improve the sensory qualities of foods.

These foods are often high in calories, fat, saturated fat, sugar and salt, whilst also being low in fibre and micronutrients. Researchers describe these foods as hyperpalatable, which means it is easy to consume too much of them and not feel full and satisfied. Processing also causes changes to the structure of foods, making them softer and easier to eat — think about how quickly you could eat a fast-food burger! However, you may start to feel hungry not long after.

A 2019 study found that 57% of the average UK diet is made up of UPF and in children and teens, this can be as high as 80%

What do UPFs do to our body?

While the research on UPF is fairly new, we do know that reducing these foods in our diet is important for improving long-term health.

Chronic diseases
Several studies have associated the overconsumption of UPF with developing several chronic diseases, such as obesity, metabolic syndrome, diabetes, cardiovascular disease, high blood pressure and some types of cancers.

Mental health
Over-reliance on UPF has also been associated with increased risk of common mental health problems, such as depression, anxiety and adverse sleep.

Gut health

Evidence shows that some emulsifiers, sweeteners and artificial colours found in UPF affect the gut microbiome and there may be an association with IBD, IBS and colorectal cancer.

Cancer

Several studies have shown a consistent significant association between UPF consumption and the risk of several types of cancers, such as colorectal, breast and pancreatic cancer.

Poor nutrition

Diets high in UPF are often much poorer quality as they are very energy-dense whilst containing less nutrients and fibre, which leaves less room in your diet for more nutritious minimally processed foods. So, decreasing the UPF food in your diet and replacing with minimally processed food can improve overall diet quality.

Researchers have categorised food into four different categories based on how processed they are. This classification system is not black and white, and some foods can fall into two categories. For example, peanut butter, which in some cases can contain many extra ingredients, such as emulsifiers, stabilisers, sugar and palm oil, but there are more natural options available that just contain nuts and salt.

It's important to note that while reducing UPF is a positive thing, not all foods classed as minimally processed are healthy foods and some UPF can still be included in a healthy diet.

Try to focus on having an overall balanced diet based around wholefoods, such as whole grains, fruit, vegetables and nuts, and reduce processed foods in your diet, especially those that are high in saturated fat and free sugars. It's all about balance, not deprivation, so you can occasionally have a packet of crisps or a bowl of cereal without worrying!

1) Unprocessed or minimally processed foods

These are foods in their whole natural form, as well as foods that have been through processes such as cooking, freezing, drying or pasteurisation. The whole foods include fruits, vegetables, herbs, nuts, seeds, legumes, meat, dried fruit, honey and eggs. This category also has foods made up of two or more ingredients from this group, such as pasta and couscous. These foods can sometimes have vitamins or minerals added to replace those lost from processing.

2) Processed culinary ingredients

These foods are used to cook and season food and may contain additives to prolong the shelf life.
Key examples: oils, butter, vinegar, sugar, salt and flour

3) Processed foods

These are foods that have been preserved with methods such as canning, bottling and non-alcoholic fermentation, as well as foods that are a combination of minimally or unprocessed foods and culinary ingredients.
Key examples: tinned vegetables or legumes, tinned fruit, tinned fish, ham, bacon, deli meats, smoked fish, most freshly baked breads and cheeses

4) Ultra-processed foods

These are industrially produced foods that are formulated using things you wouldn't find in an ordinary kitchen, such as additives, preservatives, colourings, artificial flavourings, emulsifiers and gums, to make the foods more palatable and appealing to consumers.
Key examples: carbonated drinks, ice cream, confectionery, crisps, biscuits, pastries, cakes, mass-produced bread, margarine, vegan 'meats' and 'cheeses', as well as most ready meals

Common Ultra-processed Food Swaps

COMMON ULTRA-PROCESSED FOODS	MINIMALLY PROCESSED ALTERNATIVES
Breakfast cereals, energy bars and biscuits	Porridge, homemade granola and granola bars (see pages 14, 19 and 180)
Mass-produced packaged breads	Sourdough, rye bread and homemade breads (with the focus on wholegrains) (see page 154)
Margarines and spreads	Olive oil, butter, natural almond butter or peanut butter
Fruit yogurts and fruit drinks	Natural unsweetened Greek yogurt and homemade fruit smoothies (see page 34)
Vegan 'meat' and 'cheese' alternatives	Naturally vegan meals (focusing on beans, legumes and wholegrains)
Ready meals	Homemade meals
Pre-made pasta sauce and pizza	Homemade pizza and pasta dishes (focusing on veggies and wholegrains)
Breaded and battered fish and meat products	Homemade wholegrain breaded chicken and fish
Sausages, burgers, hot dogs and other processed meat products	Homemade burger patties, tinned tuna or salmon and roasted chicken
Instant and tinned soups	Homemade soups (see pages 46, 58, 64)
Instant noodles	Meal prep noodle jars and stir-fries (see page 53)
Sweet or savoury packaged snacks, such as crisps, biscuits, pastries, cakes and ice cream	Oat crackers (see page 159), biscuits (see page 170), brownies (see page 179), granola bars (see page 180), homemade protein balls (see page 183) and popcorn (see page 184)

If you are buying stock cubes, pre-cooked rice, pre-made sauces, coconut milk, chocolate or similar ingredients try and opt for something with ingredients that you recognise and would use in your own kitchen

Breakfast & Brunch

Switching your UPF breakfast options to a minimally processed alternative is probably the easiest place to start! Things like cereals can be swapped to porridge or a homemade granola and I have included lots of options for quick and easy weekday breakfasts as well as some weekend brunch recipes.

VG

Cook time
1HR 5MIN

Makes around
6
PORTIONS

Maple Cinnamon Granola

200g oats
60g flaked almonds
60g hazelnuts, chopped
50g pecans, chopped
50g desiccated coconut
50g pumpkin seeds
80g coconut oil, melted
100ml maple syrup
1 tsp vanilla extract
1 tsp ground cinnamon
Pinch of salt

Most cereals in supermarkets are ultra-processed, so making your own granola is a good alternative option that is similar to cereal! I like to serve mine with yogurt or milk and berries and you can also use this granola as a topping for other breakfasts.

1. Preheat the oven to 170°C.

2. Mix together the oats, flaked almonds, hazelnuts, pecans, desiccated coconut, pumpkin seeds, coconut oil, maple syrup, vanilla extract, cinnamon and salt until well combined.

3. Spread the mixture evenly onto a lined baking sheet (you may need to split it between two sheets as if it is too thick, it won't cook all the way through).

4. Bake for 20–25 minutes until the granola is slightly golden.

5. Leave to cool for around 30 minutes, then break into pieces.

Cook time

30

MINUTES

Makes

2

BURRITOS

Breakfast Burritos

4 eggs
4 spring onions, chopped
1 tbsp olive oil
4 tbsp cooked black beans
4 tbsp cooked kidney beans
1 large avocado
Juice of 1 lime
Handful of chopped coriander,
  plus extra to serve
2 wholegrain tortillas
2 handfuls of cherry tomatoes,
  chopped
Salt and black pepper

If you want a bit more of an exciting breakfast than scrambled eggs on toast, try making these breakfast burritos. The eggs, avocado, beans and wholegrain tortilla provide plenty of protein, fibre and healthy fats, which will help you to stay full until lunchtime.

1. In a bowl whisk together the egg, spring onion and salt and pepper.

2. Pour the olive oil into a pan along with the egg and heat the egg gently.

3. As the egg starts to cook, scramble and then set aside.

4. In a bowl mash the black beans and kidney beans together and season with salt and pepper

5. Mash the avocado, squeeze in the lime juice and add the coriander, then season with salt and pepper.

6. Heat the tortillas for a couple of minutes in a pan and then top with the beans, avocado, scrambled egg and finally the cherry tomatoes and some more chopped coriander.

7. Fold the tortillas up to serve.

BREAKFAST & BRUNCH

Cook time

20

MINUTES

Serves

1

Porridge 3 Ways

PORRIDGE
50g oats
300–400ml milk or water
 (or use a mixture of both)
1 tbsp milled flaxseed
1 tbsp maple syrup or honey
½ tsp vanilla extract

BERRY COMPOTE
150g frozen mixed red berries
2 tbsp maple syrup or honey
½ banana, sliced
1 tbsp pumpkin seeds

CHOCOLATE PEANUT BUTTER BANANA
½ banana, sliced
2 tbsp natural peanut butter
1 tbsp shelled hemp seeds
1 tbsp grated dark chocolate

LEMON & BLUEBERRY
Juice and zest of ½ lemon
Handful of blueberries
1 tbsp shelled hemp seeds

Some people think of it as being quite a boring breakfast, but it doesn't have to be! It really is all about the toppings you add and here I have given three of my favourite variations.

1. Put the porridge oats in a saucepan along with the milk or water, milled flaxseed, maple syrup or honey and vanilla extract.

2. Bring to a simmer and cook for 5–10 minutes, stirring every little while, until the porridge thickens.

3. Place the porridge in a bowl then add your toppings.

For the berry compote
1. Put the frozen berries and maple syrup or honey in a saucepan and bring to a low heat.

2. Cook the berries for around 5–10 minutes until they have defrosted and formed a sauce.

3. Top the porridge with this and add some banana and pumpkin seeds.

For the chocolate peanut butter banana
Simply top the porridge with banana slices, peanut butter, hemp seeds and grated dark chocolate.

For the lemon & blueberry
Stir the lemon juice into the porridge and then top with blueberries, lemon zest and hemp seeds.

Cook time
30
MINUTES

Makes
12
MUFFINS

Berry Breakfast Muffins

2 large bananas
2 eggs
2 tbsp milk
1 tsp vanilla extract
4 tbsp butter, melted,
   plus extra to grease the tin
4 tbsp honey
200g buckwheat flour
50g oats
1 tsp ground cinnamon
1½ tsp baking powder
½ tsp bicarbonate of soda
100g blueberries
100g raspberries
2 tbsp pumpkin seeds
2 tbsp oats

These muffins are a really easy way to prep a healthy breakfast you can take with you on the go. I like using buckwheat flour as it adds a nutty flavour, but you can substitute it with wholewheat flour if you can't find this.

1. Preheat the oven to 180°C.

2. Mash the bananas in a bowl and add the eggs, milk, vanilla, melted butter and honey.

3. Now add the buckwheat flour, oats, cinnamon, baking powder and bicarbonate of soda and mix until combined.

4. Gently fold in the blueberries and raspberries.

5. Divide the mixture evenly into a muffin tin lined with greaseproof paper and greased with butter. Sprinkle the oats and pumpkin seeds over the top and then bake for 20–25 minutes until golden brown.

Cook time
45
MINUTES

Makes
4
PORTIONS

Meal Prep Breakfast Sandwich

1 tbsp olive oil
4 spring onions, trimmed
  and diced
½ red pepper, chopped
½ orange pepper, chopped
2 handfuls of spinach
8 eggs
Handful of chopped parsley
Handful of chopped basil
4 wholegrain bagels
Coconut oil, to grease the tin
Salt and black pepper

AVOCADO MASH
2 large avocados
Juice of 2 lemons
Handful of chopped basil
200g cherry vine tomatoes,
  chopped

This meal prep is a really easy way to make a quick and filling breakfast. The filling is basically like an egg frittata and packed with lots of spinach, peppers and herbs. When you want to eat it, all you need to do is mash an avocado and assemble the sandwich! The frittata will keep in the fridge for up to three days.

1. Preheat the oven to 180°C.

2. Pour the oil into a pan and add the spring onion, red pepper, orange pepper and spinach. Cook for a few minutes until the vegetables start to soften.

3. Whisk the eggs together in a bowl and then add in the parsley, basil, salt, pepper and the vegetables you just cooked. Pour this into a greased square tin and bake for around 20–25 minutes until golden brown on top and the egg is set.

4. Leave to cool down and then slice into four pieces and store in the fridge.

5. When you want to assemble a sandwich, mash half an avocado, add in the juice of ½ a lemon, some chopped basil and 50g cherry tomatoes and mix together.

Cook time

20
MINUTES

Makes
12
COOKIES

Blueberry Breakfast Cookies

2 bananas
100ml milk
3 tbsp natural peanut butter
200g oats
2 tbsp milled flaxseed
100g blueberries
50g dark chocolate chips

If you are looking for an easy make-ahead breakfast you can take with you to work or school, then these cookies are the perfect option. You can switch the blueberries to any other berries you like or even use frozen berries to make these cookies all year round.

1. Preheat the oven to 180°C and line a baking tray with baking paper.

2. Mash the bananas until smooth and then add the milk and peanut butter and stir to combine.

3. Add in the oats and milled flaxseed and mix together.

4. Gently mix in the blueberries and chocolate chips.

5. Shape into 12 equally-sized cookies and then bake for 12–14 minutes until golden.

6. These cookies will last for a few days in an airtight container.

V

Cook time
25
MINUTES

Serves
4

Oat & Greek Yogurt Pancakes

2 bananas
250g oats
250g Greek yogurt
250ml milk
1 tsp baking powder
Coconut oil or butter
   to grease the pan

TOPPINGS
Maple syrup
Berries

I really love using oats to make pancakes because it's like having a bowl of porridge in pancake form. These pancakes can be stored in the fridge or even frozen and then heated up in a toaster or pan for a really quick and easy breakfast!

1. Place the banana, oats, Greek yogurt, milk and baking powder in a blender and blend until smooth.

2. Heat a non-stick pan with a little coconut oil or butter and then scoop in the pancake mix. I use around ¼ cup per pancake. If the pancake batter is too runny, leave it to sit for around 10–15 minutes to thicken.

3. Cook the pancakes on both sides until golden brown and then serve with maple syrup and berries.

Cook time

40
MINUTES

Serves
4

Healthier Cooked Breakfast

BREAKFAST
300g chestnut mushrooms, halved
400g cherry vine tomatoes
3 tbsp olive oil
1 garlic clove, minced
1 tsp dried thyme
8 sausages
4 eggs
Salt and black pepper

HASH BROWNS
4 Maris Piper potatoes
1 white onion
1 egg
1–2 tbsp olive oil

TO SERVE
Batch of Spiced Baked Beans (Optional, see page 43)
2 avocados, halved
Cress

If you are looking for non-UPF sausages and bacon, then I would recommend buying them from a local butcher as these are much fresher and tend to not have as many additives as the ones you typically find in supermarkets.

1. Preheat the oven to 200°C.

2. Place the mushrooms and cherry tomatoes in a roasting tin, drizzle over 2 tablespoons of the olive oil and sprinkle over garlic and thyme.

3. Roast for 12 minutes until the mushrooms and tomatoes are soft. Cook your sausages according to the package directions.

4. Meanwhile, grate the potatoes and onion onto a clean tea towel and then squeeze out the liquid.

5. Add the egg, season with salt and pepper, then mix together.

6. Heat a pan with a bit of olive oil, add spoonfuls of the potato mixture and flatten these. Cook for around 2–3 minutes on each side until they are crispy and then set aside.

7. In another pan add in another tablespoon of olive oil. Crack your eggs into a bowl, season with salt and pepper and whisk together then pour into a pan and scramble them.

Sourdough French Toast

2 eggs
250ml oat milk
1 tbsp maple syrup
1 tsp vanilla extract
2 tsp ground cinnamon
1 tbsp butter
8 slices of sourdough bread
(see tip)

TOPPINGS
Maple syrup
Berries
Greek yogurt

TIP
When choosing your bread, try and choose one just made with flour, salt, water and a sourdough starter (add-ins such as seeds and wholemeal or rye flour are fine too!). Some supermarkets sell 'sourdough-style' bread, which can be ultra-processed and makes it confusing. Alternatively, you can find sourdough bread in a local bakery or make it yourself!

Using sourdough in place of processed bread can be an easy non-ultra-processed swap. Some people even find sourdough easier to digest, though contrary to popular belief, this is not due to gluten but instead to the longer fermentation process used, which breaks down the carbohydrates in the wheat.

1. In a shallow bowl, whisk together the eggs, oat milk, maple syrup, vanilla extract and cinnamon.

2. Meanwhile, heat the butter in a non-stick pan.

3. Dip a slice of bread in the egg mixture, flip to coat both sides and then transfer to the pan. Don't leave the bread in the egg mixture too long or it will get too soggy and break.

4. Cook the bread on both sides for a couple of minutes until golden. Repeat with all the slices of bread.

5. Serve the French toast topped with maple syrup and berries and yogurt.

Sweetcorn Fritters

SWEETCORN FRITTERS

285g tin of sweetcorn, drained

2 eggs

100g plain flour

1 tsp baking powder

8 spring onions, trimmed and
finely sliced, reserving some
for the top

2 tbsp chopped chives, plus
extra for the top

Pinch of chilli powder

Salt and pepper, to taste

1 tbsp olive oil

SALSA

1 large avocado, chopped

Handful of cherry vine
tomatoes, chopped

Juice of ½ lime

Handful of chopped coriander

Pinch of chilli flakes

**I'm always looking for more savoury breakfast options
and these sweetcorn fritters are quick and easy to
make. If you want to make this breakfast higher
in protein, then I would recommend adding some
scrambled or poached eggs along with the salsa to
top them!**

1. Mix together the sweetcorn, eggs, plain flour,
   baking powder, spring onion, chopped chives, chilli
   powder, salt and pepper in a bowl until combined.

2. Heat a non-stick pan with a little bit of oil and scoop
   even-sized portions of the batter into the pan in
   circle shapes. I like to use around ¼ cup of batter
   for each fritter.

3. Cook the fritters on both sides until they start to
   turn golden brown and are fully cooked through.
   Repeat with all the batter.

4. Meanwhile to make the salsa, combine the
   avocado, cherry tomatoes, lime juice, coriander and
   chilli flakes in a bowl.

5. To serve, top the fritters with the salsa and some
   chopped chives and spring onion.

BREAKFAST & BRUNCH

V

Cook time
5
MINUTES

Serves
2

Berry Breakfast Smoothie

2 frozen bananas
300g frozen blueberries,
  raspberries and strawberries
2 tbsp milled flaxseed
2 shelled hemp seeds
4 tbsp oats
300ml milk

A smoothie can be a great quick and easy option for breakfast. I like to include seeds such as milled flaxseed and hemp seeds, as well as oats to add in complex carbohydrates, healthy fats and a bit of protein to help you stay feeling full.

1. Place all the ingredients in a blender and blend until completely smooth.

TIP
Use frozen fruit in your smoothies as this helps to create a thick and creamy texture and allows you to include berries in your diet, even in colder months.

Quick, Make-Ahead Lunch

A lot of common lunch options, such as sandwiches, soups and even some salads from supermarkets, are ultra-processed. Prepping your lunches and having quick and easy go-to options is a straightforward way to stick to healthier, non-ultra-processed meals. I have included some options that you can make ahead, some quick and easy ones and lunches that you can take with you to work.

Sweet Potato & Quinoa Lunchboxes

2 large sweet potatoes, chopped
1 tbsp olive oil
2 sprigs of rosemary, chopped
400g tin of chickpeas, drained and rinsed
400g cooked quinoa
1 avocado
4 tbsp hummus (see page 160)
2 tbsp sesame seeds
Salt and black pepper

Pre-making your lunches makes it much easier to reduce UPFs in your diet. I really like to focus on grains and roasted vegetables to add in lots of fibre. You can switch up the vegetables or grains every week as this is a good way to add diversity to your diet, which is great for gut health!

1. Preheat your oven to 200°C.

2. Put the sweet potato on a baking tray, drizzle over olive oil and sprinkle over salt, pepper and the rosemary.

3. Roast in the oven for 20–25 minutes until the potatoes are soft and golden brown.

4. Add in the chickpeas and mix to coat in the oil, then return to the oven for another 10 minutes.

5. Place the quinoa, sweet potato and chickpeas in two lunchboxes or serving bowls.

6. Slice the avocado in half, peel off the skin and add that to the boxes with a dollop of hummus and a sprinkle of sesame seeds.

Spiced Baked Beans on Toast

1 tbsp olive oil
1 onion, finely diced
2 garlic cloves, minced
1 tbsp tomato paste
½ tsp smoked paprika
¼ tsp dried thyme
1 tbsp soy sauce
2 x 400g tins of haricot beans, drained
200g passata
Salt and black pepper

TO SERVE
Toasted sourdough bread
½ avocado, sliced
Chopped chives
Chilli flakes (optional)

Beans on toast is a really classic breakfast or lunch, but the beans in the supermarket often have a lot of added sugar and salt. Making them at home means you can reduce this and add more flavour!

1. In a pan, heat the oil, add in the onion and cook for a few minutes until soft.

2. Once this is done, add in the garlic and tomato paste and continue cooking for a couple more minutes.

3. Now add in smoked paprika, thyme, soy sauce, drained haricot beans and passata and season with salt and pepper.

4. Simmer gently for 15–20 minutes until the sauce has thickened.

5. Serve with toast and top with avocado, chives and chilli flakes, if using.

Leek, Asparagus & Pea Frittata

500g baby potatoes
8 eggs
100ml milk
50g mature Cheddar cheese, grated, reserving some for the top
50g vegetarian Italian hard cheese, grated, reserving some for the top
2 tsp Dijon mustard
1 tsp wholegrain mustard
1 tbsp olive oil
2 leeks, washed, trimmed and chopped
200g asparagus, trimmed and cut into small pieces
200g frozen peas, defrosted
Salt and black pepper

TO SERVE
Chopped parsley

This is the perfect thing to meal prep on the weekend if you want a lunch to take to work that is a bit different to a sandwich and can be eaten cold or even as an easy dinner! You can switch up the vegetables in the frittata depending on what is in season.

1. Preheat the oven to 180°C.

2. Heat a pan of water and boil the baby potatoes for around 5 minutes until slightly soft, then slice.

3. In a large bowl, mix together the eggs, milk, Cheddar and Italian hard cheeses, Dijon and wholegrain mustards and season with salt and pepper.

4. Meanwhile, heat the oil in a pan and cook the leek for a few minutes until soft.

5. Add in the asparagus, peas and baby potatoes, then pour over the egg mixture.

6. Top with the reserved cheese and then bake for around 20–25 minutes until the frittata is no longer runny and it is golden brown on top.

7. To serve, top with fresh parsley and eat with a side salad.

V

Cook time

1

HOUR

Serves

4

Creamy Tomato Soup

1.5kg tomatoes, chopped
(I use a mix of big and cherry
tomatoes)
2 red peppers, chopped
3 tbsp olive oil
2 tbsp balsamic vinegar
½ tsp chilli flakes, plus extra
for the top
1 tsp Italian herbs
1 onion, finely chopped
3 garlic cloves
4 tbsp tomato paste
500ml vegetable or chicken
stock
200g crème fraîche, plus extra
for the top
Large handful of chopped basil,
plus extra for the top
Salt and black pepper

Making a batch of soup for lunches or dinners is such a quick and easy option and a great way to add more veggies into your diet. If you want to turn your soup into a more filling meal, pair with some wholegrain or sourdough bread.

1. Preheat the oven to 200°C.

2. Put the tomatoes and peppers into a roasting tin, drizzle over 2 tablespoons of the olive oil and balsamic vinegar, sprinkle over chilli flakes and Italian herbs and season with salt and pepper.

3. Roast the tomatoes for around 30–35 minutes until they are soft, stirring halfway through to make sure they get evenly cooked.

4. Meanwhile, in a pan over medium heat fry the onion in the remaining olive oil until soft.

5. Add in the garlic and tomato paste and cook for a couple more minutes.

6. Then add in the roasted tomatoes and red pepper, the stock, crème fraîche and a handful of fresh basil and mix to combine.

7. Let this simmer for around 10–15 minutes to let everything combine.

8. Blend the soup until smooth and then serve topped with some more crème fraîche, chilli flakes and fresh basil!

Cook time
15
MINUTES

Serves
2

Coronation Chicken Salad

5 heaped tbsp Greek yogurt
2 tsp curry powder
½ tsp ground turmeric
1 tsp mango chutney
Juice of 1 lemon
150g shredded roast chicken
2 tbsp sultanas
2 tbsp chopped spring onion,
    plus extra for the top
120g mixed green salad (I used
    a baby green lettuce, spinach,
    baby red lettuce, chard mix)

TO SERVE
Toasted flaked almonds

Coronation chicken is such a classic filling for sandwiches and jacket potatoes and is a great way to use up leftover chicken to make a protein-packed lunch. You can prep the coronation chicken the day before for an even quicker lunch option.

1. In a bowl, mix together the Greek yogurt, curry powder, turmeric, mango chutney and lemon juice.

2. Reserve 2 tablespoons of the dressing to top the salad, then mix the rest of the dressing with the chicken, sultanas and chopped spring onion.

3. Divide the mixed green salad between two bowls and place spoonfuls of the chicken mixture on top.

4. Drizzle over the remaining dressing and sprinkle over toasted flaked almonds and more spring onion.

Egg Salad Sandwiches

EGG FILLING
4 eggs
4 tbsp Greek yogurt
1 tsp Dijon mustard
Juice of ½ lemon
2 tbsp chopped chives
2 tbsp chopped dill
5 spring onions, trimmed and
   chopped
Salt and black pepper

SANDWICH
4 slices of sourdough bread
Baby leaf mixed green salad
Cherry vine tomatoes, halved

This protein-packed twist on a classic makes the perfect picnic or lunch sandwich and is so easy to make! I love adding the Dijon mustard and fresh chives, dill and spring onions to my egg salad to give lots of flavour and freshness.

1. Bring a pan of water to a gentle boil, add in the eggs and boil for 10 minutes.

2. Once they are done, plunge them into ice-cold water and leave for 3–5 minutes.

3. Peel the eggs, roughly chop them, and then place them in a bowl.

4. To the bowl add the Greek yogurt, Dijon mustard, lemon juice, chives, dill and spring onion and season with salt and pepper. Mix until combined.

5. To assemble the sandwiches, spread the egg filling on two slices of sourdough bread, then top with the mixed green salad, cherry tomatoes and the other slices of bread.

Cook time

15

MINUTES

Makes

3

JARS

Meal Prep Noodle Jars

150g soba noodles

3 tbsp soy sauce

2 tsp toasted sesame oil

3 tsp miso paste

3 handfuls of shredded red cabbage

3 large carrot, julienned

2 red peppers, diced

3 cooked chicken breasts, shredded

150g cooked edamame

3 chopped spring onions

Noodles are often thought of as an unhealthy meal, but they really don't have to be! For these jars I use soba noodles, which are made from buckwheat and add a nutty flavour, plus some layers of vegetables as well as edamame and shredded chicken to add in lots of protein.

1. Cook the noodles according to the package directions and then rinse with cold water and set aside.

2. Put the soy sauce, sesame oil and miso paste in a bowl and mix until evenly combined. You may need to add water if it is too thick.

3. Divide this sauce evenly among the three jars and then divide the noodles evenly among the jars.

4. Now layer the red cabbage, carrot, red pepper, shredded chicken, edamame and spring onion.

5. The jars can be stored in the fridge for a few days. To serve, tip into a bowl and then mix to fully coat in the sauce.

Pesto Pasta Salad

BASIL PESTO

60g basil leaves

50g pine nuts

Juice of 1 lemon

60ml olive oil

30g vegetarian Italian
  hard cheese

2–3 garlic cloves, peeled

Pinch of sea salt and black
  pepper

PASTA SALAD

400g wholewheat pasta

150g cherry vine tomatoes,
  halved

4 tbsp pine nuts

I always use this basil pesto in my recipes because it's so easy to make and tastes so much fresher than the pesto you can buy in supermarkets! This pesto should last for a few days, stored in the fridge, if you want to prep it to use in other recipes.

1. Put the basil, pine nuts, lemon juice, olive oil, cheese, garlic, salt and pepper in a food processor and blend.

2. Cook your pasta according to the package directions and then leave to cool.

3. Once it is cool, mix in the pesto and divide among four lunchboxes or containers.

4. Top with the cherry tomatoes and pine nuts.

Cook time

30

MINUTES

Serves

2

Steak Burrito Bowl

150g brown rice
1 tbsp olive oil
½ onion, chopped
1–2 red and orange or yellow
  peppers, sliced
250g steak strips
½ tsp smoked paprika
½ tsp chilli powder
½ tsp ground cumin
½ tsp dried oregano
Handful of chopped coriander
Juice of 1 lime
2 roasted corn cobs, kernels
  removed
150g cooked black beans
Salt and black pepper

**AVOCADO MASH AND
CHERRY TOMATOES**
1 avocado
Juice of 1 lime
Handful of chopped coriander
1 tbsp olive oil
150g cherry vine tomatoes,
  halved

**This burrito bowl is packed full of flavour and makes
a really filling lunch. If you prep the brown rice in
advance, this bowl will only take around 30 minutes
to make or you could also use some precooked rice for
an even quicker meal.**

1. Cook the brown rice according to the package
    directions, then set aside.

2. Put the olive oil, onion and peppers in a pan and
    cook for around 5 minutes.

3. Add in the steak strips, smoked paprika, chilli
    powder, cumin and oregano, season with salt and
    pepper and cook for around 8–10 minutes until the
    steak is cooked, then set aside.

4. Meanwhile, mix the rice with the coriander and lime
    juice and add this to a bowl.

5. Mash the avocado and mix in the juice of ½ the
    lime, half the coriander, a bit of oil and some salt
    and pepper.

6. Mix the cherry tomatoes with the remaining
    coriander and the rest of the lime juice.

7. Start with a base of rice in two bowls, and then top
    with roasted corn, black beans, cherry tomatoes,
    the steak and pepper mix and mashed avocado.

Three Bean Chilli Soup

1 tbsp olive oil
1 large onion, finely chopped
2 carrots, grated
2 garlic cloves, crushed
1 red pepper, chopped
4 tbsp tomato paste
2 tsp chilli powder
1 tsp ground cumin
2 tsp smoked paprika
2 x 400g tins of chopped
   tomatoes
1 litre vegetable stock
400g tin of kidney beans,
   drained and rinsed
400g tin of black beans,
   drained and rinsed
400g tin of black eye beans,
   drained and rinsed

TO SERVE
4 tbsp sour cream
Chilli flakes
Chopped coriander

This bean soup is such a comforting and filling meal with all the beans and spices. It is the perfect thing to prep to eat on a cold day. Beans are something we want to be eating more of as they are high in fibre, iron and other nutrients and are great for gut health.

1. Put the olive oil and onion in a pan and cook for a few minutes until soft and then add in the grated carrot, garlic and red pepper.

2. Continue cooking for around 5 minutes until this starts to soften.

3. Add in the tomato paste, chilli powder, cumin and smoked paprika and cook for a couple of minutes until this becomes fragrant.

4. Add in the chopped tomatoes, vegetable stock, kidney beans, black beans and black eye beans.

5. Bring this to a gentle simmer and let it simmer for around 30 minutes to allow everything to cook together and thicken slightly.

6. To serve, top with sour cream and sprinkle over the chilli flakes and coriander.

7. This soup can also be stored in the fridge for a few days or frozen for meal prepping.

Cook time

10
MINUTES

Serves
1

Avocado & Tomato Tuna Melt

145g tin of tuna, drained
2 tbsp Greek yogurt
1 tsp Dijon mustard
1 tbsp capers, chopped
1 tbsp chopped chives, plus
extra for the top
Salt and black pepper

TO SERVE
2 slices of sourdough bread
1 avocado, mashed
4 tomato slices
4 tbsp grated Cheddar cheese

If you are looking for an easy lunch to make while working at home that is high in protein, then try this easy tuna melt. Tuna is a really affordable source of protein and is also a good source of B vitamins, calcium and vitamin D.

1. Mix together the tuna, Greek yogurt, mustard, capers, chives and salt and pepper until combined.

2. Layer a piece of bread with mashed avocado, tomato and the tuna mixture and top with grated cheese.

3. Grill until the cheese is melted. Serve topped with chives.

Meal Prep Salad Jars

2 tbsp olive oil
1 tbsp lemon juice
½ large cucumber, chopped
150g cherry vine tomatoes, chopped
1 red onion, chopped
400g tin of chickpeas, drained and rinsed
400g cooked quinoa
3 tbsp chopped coriander
3 large handfuls of rocket
Salt and black pepper

These jars are the easiest way to prep a salad for lunch that won't go soggy as the dressing sits at the bottom away from the salad leaves. You can switch up the veggies and grains to what is in season or any leftovers you have from other meals to prevent food waste!

1. Divide the olive oil and lemon juice between the jars and season with salt and pepper.

2. Divide the cucumber, tomato, red onion, chickpeas and quinoa between the jars evenly. Top the with the coriander and rocket.

3. The jars can be stored in the fridge for a few days.

4. To serve, tip into a bowl and mix so the dressing evenly coats everything.

Carrot, Coconut & Lentil Soup

1 tbsp olive oil
1 onion
2 garlic cloves, grated
1 tbsp curry powder
1 tsp ground turmeric
1 tsp ground cumin
1 tsp chilli flakes
200g lentils
600g carrots, grated
1 litre vegetable stock
400ml tin of coconut milk
Salt and black pepper

TOPPINGS
Coconut cream
Chilli flakes
Chopped coriander

I really love having recipes like this on hand that use mostly cupboard staples and don't require too many fresh ingredients. The lentils add protein and fibre to make it filling and it costs less than £5 to make 4 portions.

1. Heat a pan with the olive oil and add in the onion, then cook for a few minutes.

2. Once the onion is softened, add in the garlic and continue cooking for a couple more minutes.

3. Add in the curry powder, turmeric, cumin and chilli flakes and stir. Let this cook for a couple more minutes until it becomes fragrant.

4. Stir in the lentils, carrot, vegetable stock and coconut milk and let this simmer for 15–20 minutes until the carrots and lentils are cooked, then season with salt and pepper.

5. Blend the soup until smooth and top with coconut cream, chilli flakes and coriander.

VG

Cook time
1HR15MIN

Serves
4

Chickpea Curry Jacket Potatoes

4 baking potatoes, washed
2 tbsp olive oil, plus extra
for the potatoes
1 onion, diced
2 garlic cloves, minced
1 thumb-sized piece of fresh
ginger, chopped
1 tsp chilli flakes
1 tsp ground coriander
2 tsp ground cumin
1 tsp ground turmeric
2 tbsp garam masala
2 x 400g tins of chickpeas,
drained and rinsed
2 x 400g tins of chopped
tomatoes
400ml coconut milk
Salt and black pepper

TOPPINGS
Chopped coriander
Chilli flakes

If you are looking for a new jacket potato filling, then try out this easy and prepable chickpea curry. Try eating food with lots of herbs and spices as many contain antioxidants and other compounds that may help to improve health, as well as just making food taste good!

1. Preheat the oven to 200°C.

2. Pierce all the potatoes with a fork, place in a roasting tin, drizzle with olive oil and sprinkle over salt and pepper.

3. Place in the oven for 45 minutes–1 hour until the skin is crispy and the potatoes are soft in the middle.

4. Meanwhile, heat the olive oil in a pan, add the onion and cook for a few minutes until softened.

5. Add in garlic, ginger, chilli flakes, ground coriander, cumin, turmeric and garam masala and cook for a couple of minutes until fragrant.

6. Add in the chickpeas, chopped tomatoes and coconut milk and leave to simmer gently for 25–30 minutes until everything has come together and it has thickened slightly.

7. Once the potatoes are done, slice in half and top with the chickpea curry. Sprinkle over the coriander and chilli flakes to serve.

Everyday Classics

I have picked recipes for this chapter that are really popular restaurant meals, ready meals and meals that commonly contain ultra-processed ingredients. I've then made changes to make them slightly healthier and to remove any UPFs.

Roasted Tomato Gnocchi

Gnocchi is a favourite of mine, and this sauce is so delicious! Gnocchi is probably the easiest pasta to make and it literally only requires potatoes, egg, plain flour and salt. I have also used this recipe to make sweet potato gnocchi!

GNOCCHI
1kg potatoes
200g plain flour
½ tsp salt
1 egg

ROASTED TOMATO SAUCE
1 tbsp olive oil
12 large tomatoes, quartered
2 garlic cloves, minced
2 tsp dried oregano
1 tsp chilli flakes
3 tbsp balsamic vinegar
200g sun-dried tomatoes,
    drained and chopped
Large handful of chopped basil,
    reserving some for the top

TO SERVE
4 tbsp pine nuts

1. Preheat your oven to 200°C.

2. Place the potatoes on a baking tray and pierce with a fork. Bake the potatoes for 1 hour until they are soft and fully cooked through.

3. Once the potatoes are cool, peel them and mix in the flour, salt and egg and bring together into a ball with your hands. Knead for 1–2 minutes. Divide into six pieces, roll into 2cm-wide logs and then cut the logs into small pieces.

4. Meanwhile, reduce the oven temperature to 180°C and put the olive oil, tomatoes, garlic, oregano, chilli flakes and balsamic vinegar in a roasting tin, mix together and cook for around 25 minutes.

5. Gently toast the pine nuts in a dry frying pan for 1 minute, then set aside.

6. Bring a pan of water to a boil and cook the gnocchi for around 1 minute or until they float to the surface.

7. Put the roasted tomatoes, sun-dried tomatoes and fresh basil in a pan and mix, then heat through for a couple of minutes, before mixing in the gnocchi. Serve with basil and pine nuts sprinkled on top.

Cook time
1HR **30**MIN

Serves
4–6

Beef & Lentil Cottage Pie

2 tbsp olive oil
1 onion, finely chopped
3 garlic cloves, minced
500g beef mince
200g carrots, grated
200g celery sticks, chopped
200g chestnut mushrooms,
   finely chopped
2 tbsp plain flour
400g tin of green lentils,
   drained and rinsed
1 tbsp chopped thyme, plus
   extra for the top
1 tbsp chopped rosemary
2 bay leaves
500ml vegetable stock
2 tbsp Worcestershire sauce
1 tbsp wholegrain mustard
1 tbsp Dijon mustard
Salt and black pepper

MASH
1.5kg potatoes, peeled and
   chopped
2 tbsp butter
125ml milk

I like to add lots of veggies and lentils to my cottage pie as this gives extra nutrients and fibre, as well as helping to bulk it out a bit and make this an affordable dish! This is another meal that can freeze really well, so it is really perfect for meal prepping.

1. Put a bit of oil in a pan and then cook the onion until it is soft for a few minutes. Add in the garlic and cook this for a couple more minutes. Add in the beef mince and cook for around 5–8 minutes to brown it. Add the grated carrot, celery and mushrooms and let this cook for 5–10 minutes until they start to soften

2. Now add in the rest of the ingredients, then let this simmer gently for around 30–40 minutes until the sauce has thickened.

3. Meanwhile, bring a pan of water to the boil and boil your potatoes for 10–15 minutes until soft and then drain.

4. Mash the potatoes, adding butter, milk and salt and pepper.

5. Add your cottage pie filling to a dish, then top your pie with the potato and smooth with a fork. Bake for 20–25 minutes until the top starts to turn golden brown.

6. Top with fresh thyme to serve.

Classic Spaghetti Bolognese

1 tbsp olive oil
1 large onion, finely chopped
3 carrots, grated
2 garlic cloves, crushed
250g mushrooms, finely chopped
500g beef mince
2 x 400g tins of chopped tomatoes
500ml vegetable stock
2 tsp Italian herbs
½ tsp chilli flakes
4 tbsp tomato paste
400g wholewheat spaghetti or pasta of choice
Salt and black pepper

TO SERVE
Chopped basil
Pine nuts
Grated Parmesan cheese

Bolognese is a classic family weeknight meal and this one has some hidden veggies in the sauce. Make sure your onion, carrots and mushrooms are really finely chopped when making this recipe so they can cook into the sauce!

1. Heat a bit of oil in a pan and add in the chopped onion.

2. Cook this for around 5 minutes until the onion starts to soften and then add in the grated carrot, garlic and mushrooms.

3. Continue to cook this for around 10 more minutes until the veggies have reduced in size.

4. Add in the beef mince and cook for around 10 minutes until browned.

5. Add in the chopped tomatoes, stock, Italian herbs, chilli flakes and tomato paste.

6. Let the sauce simmer for around 1 hour until everything is nicely combined, then season with salt and pepper.

7. Cook the spaghetti according to the package directions and then stir into the sauce.

8. Serve topped with fresh basil, pine nuts and grated Parmesan.

Traybake Roast Chicken

6 large potatoes, chopped
400g Chantenay carrots
200g parsnips, chopped
1.5kg whole chicken
4 tbsp olive oil
2 tbsp honey
2 tbsp chopped thyme
2 tbsp chopped rosemary
1 lemon
Salt and black pepper

This traybake is such an easy option to put together for a Sunday roast or a weeknight meal. I love making this on the weekend so I have some leftover roasted chicken that I can shred to use for the rest of the week to make salads for lunch or in other recipes.

1. Preheat the oven to 200°C.

2. Put the potatoes, carrots and parsnips in a roasting tin in one layer and place the chicken on top.

3. Drizzle over the olive oil and honey and sprinkle over the thyme, rosemary and salt and pepper. Place the lemon inside the chicken.

4. Roast the chicken for 1 hour 20 minutes until the chicken is golden and the juices run clear.

5. Serve with some steamed vegetables.

Chicken Pad Thai

400g chicken, chopped into strips
4 tbsp chopped coriander
Salt and black pepper
1 tbsp coconut oil
180g rice noodles
2 garlic cloves, minced
Bunch of spring onions, trimmed and chopped
200g beansprouts
4 tbsp fish sauce
2 tbsp tamarind paste
1 tbsp tomato paste
2 tsp sambal oelek
1 tbsp brown sugar
2 tbsp chopped roasted peanuts
Juice of 1 lime

TO SERVE
Sliced red chilli
Chopped spring onion
Chopped coriander
Chopped roasted peanuts

I love using rice noodles for midweek meals because they cook so quickly. For this recipe you can swap the protein source for what suits your diet best. Prawns or tofu would work really well – just make sure to reduce the cooking time slightly.

1. Put your chicken in a bowl and sprinkle over the chopped coriander and salt and pepper, then transfer to a pan with a bit of oil and cook for around 5 minutes.

2. Meanwhile, cook the rice noodles according to the package directions.

3. Add the garlic, spring onion and beansprouts to the pan and in a bowl mix together the fish sauce, tamarind paste, tomato paste, sambal oelek and brown sugar and then add this to the chicken and beansprouts.

4. Cook this for a few more minutes and then stir in your cooked rice noodles, chopped peanuts and lime juice, then let this heat through until the chicken is fully cooked.

5. Serve topped with sliced red chilli, spring onion, coriander and roasted peanuts.

Cook time
1HR **30**MIN

Serves
4

Smoky Stuffed Peppers

1 tbsp olive oil
1 onion, chopped
2 garlic cloves
2 tbsp tomato paste
1 tsp dried oregano
1 tsp smoked paprika
1 tsp ground cumin
500g beef mince
250g cooked brown rice
6 red, yellow and orange
   peppers
100g grated mozzarella or
   Cheddar cheese

TO SERVE
Chopped parsley

Stuffed peppers are something I had for dinner a lot growing up. To make this recipe even quicker on really busy days, you can make the filling the night before and then just fill the peppers and bake them when you want to make dinner!

1. Preheat the oven to 180°C.

2. Heat a bit of oil in a pan and add in the chopped onion.

3. Cook this for around 5 minutes until the onion starts to soften and then add in the garlic and tomato paste, oregano, smoked paprika and cumin and cook for a couple more minutes.

4. Add in the beef mince and cook, breaking up the meat with a wooden spoon, for around 5 minutes.

5. Add in the cooked rice and continue cooking for 5–10 minutes until the mince is cooked.

6. Meanwhile, slice all the peppers in half and scoop out the seeds.

7. Place them in a roasting tin and fill with the rice and beef mixture, then top with cheese.

8. Bake the peppers for 25–30 minutes until the peppers are soft and the cheese is melted.

9. To serve, top with chopped parsley and I serve mine with a side salad and roasted baby potatoes.

TIP
If you are using pre-cooked brown rice for this recipe, make sure to check it doesn't contain any additives or preservatives.

EVERYDAY CLASSICS

Chicken, Leek & Mushroom Pie

ROUGH PUFF PASTRY
250g strong white flour
250g butter
Pinch of salt
150ml cold water

PIE FILLING
1 tbsp olive oil
3 leeks, washed, trimmed and chopped
2 garlic cloves, minced
300g chestnut mushrooms, sliced
3 tbsp plain flour
1 tbsp chopped sage
1 tbsp chopped thyme, plus extra for the top
500ml vegetable stock
250ml crème fraîche
1 tbsp Dijon mustard
1 tbsp wholegrain mustard
Juice of ½ lemon
4 cooked chicken breasts, shredded
1 egg, beaten

Making rough puff pastry is probably the easiest way to make your own flaky pastry for pies and other recipes at home. Many store-bought puff pastries don't use butter, so just don't taste as good, and also contain additives and even colouring, which just isn't necessary.

1. Put the flour, butter and salt in a bowl and then rub the butter and flour together, leaving some larger chunks of butter. This is key to making the pastry puff up.

2. Pour in the cold water, bring the dough together and leave in the fridge for 30 minutes.

3. Roll the dough out until it is around 1cm thick, fold into thirds and then turn the dough by a quarter turn and roll and fold this again. Repeat this step once more.

4. Place the dough back in the fridge for 30 more minutes.

5. Preheat the oven to 200°C.

6. In a large pan heat the oil, add in the leeks and cook for a few minutes until soft.

continues overleaf

Chicken, Leek
& Mushroom Pie *continued*

7. Add in the garlic and mushrooms and cook for 5–10 minutes until the mushrooms have reduced in size.

8. Then stir in the flour to coat the mushrooms and leeks.

9. Add the sage, thyme, vegetable stock, crème fraîche, Dijon and wholegrain mustards, then mix together and season with salt and pepper.

10. Let this simmer for around 15–20 minutes stirring every little while so there are no lumps until the sauce has thickened. Stir in the lemon juice and shredded chicken.

11. Lightly flour a surface and roll out the pastry so that it will be large enough to cover the top of the pie. Aim to make it no thicker than a pound coin.

12. Transfer the sauce to an ovenproof dish and top with a sheet of puff pastry. Use a fork to seal the edges and score the pastry on top. Make a small hole in the middle so any steam can escape.

13. Brush with the beaten egg and then bake for around 20-25 minutes until the pastry is golden.

14. Serve topped with fresh thyme and with some potatoes, green beans and broccoli.

Roasted Mediterranean Vegetable Lasagne

1 red pepper, sliced
1 yellow pepper, sliced
1 large aubergine, sliced
2 courgettes, sliced
1 red onion, sliced
2 garlic cloves, minced
2 tbsp olive oil
2 tsp Italian herbs
1 tsp chilli flakes
2 x 400g tins of cherry
   tomatoes
4 tbsp extra virgin olive oil
2 heaped tbsp plain flour
700ml semi-skimmed milk
60g vegetarian Italian hard
   cheese, grated, reserving
   some for the top.
60g mature Cheddar cheese,
   grated, reserving some for
   the top
Salt and black pepper
200g lasagne sheets

TO SERVE
Chopped basil

Lasagne is one of the first dishes I cooked for my family when I was younger. I really love this vegetarian version, with the layers of roasted vegetables and wholegrain pasta topped off with a creamy olive oil béchamel sauce! Use a vegetarian alternative to Parmesan if you are cooking for vegetarians.

1. Preheat the oven to 200°C.

2. Put the red and yellow peppers, aubergine, courgette, red onion and garlic in a roasting tin, drizzle over half the olive oil and sprinkle over the Italian herbs, chilli flakes and some salt and pepper.

3. Roast in the oven for around 30 minutes until the vegetables are softened and golden.

4. Add the roasted vegetables to a pan and mix in the tins of cherry tomatoes.

5. Let this simmer for around 15 minutes.

6. Meanwhile, put the remaining olive oil and flour in another pan and cook for a couple of minutes.

continues overleaf

Roasted Mediterranean Vegetable Lasagne *continued*

7. Gradually add the milk and continue stirring so there are no lumps.

8. Let this cook for around 5–10 minutes, then add in the cheeses and let them melt into the sauce.

9. In an ovenproof dish, start with a thin layer of the tomatoes and vegetables, then layer up the lasagne sheets, half the tomato and vegetable mixture, then another layer of pasta and the rest of the tomato and vegetable mixture.

10. Top with a final layer of pasta, then the béchamel sauce, and add the remaining cheese over the top.

11. Bake for 35 minutes until golden and bubbling and top with some fresh basil to serve.

Cook time

1HR **30**MIN

Serves
4

Pan-fried Beef Burgers

KETCHUP
1 tbsp olive oil
1 onion, chopped
2 x 400g tins of chopped
   tomatoes
2 tbsp honey
2 tbsp apple cider vinegar
2 tbsp tomato paste
1 tsp smoked paprika
Salt and black pepper

BURGERS
500g beef mince
½ onion, finely chopped
1 egg
1 tbsp olive oil

ROLLS AND TOPPINGS
4 slices of mature Cheddar
   cheese
4 sourdough rolls
1 beef tomato, sliced
1 gem lettuce, sliced

Try making your own ketchup and easy beef burger patties for your next BBQ. The ketchup needs to be simmered for a while and can be made in advance. You might want to try it out with other meals at home too!

1. Heat a pan with the olive oil and onion and cook for around 5 minutes until they start to soften.

2. Add in the chopped tomatoes, honey, apple cider vinegar, tomato paste, smoked paprika and salt and pepper and stir.

3. Let this simmer gently for around 40 minutes until the sauce thickens.

4. Let it cool down and then blend in a food processor or blender.

5. To make the burgers, mix the beef mince in a bowl with the onion, egg and some salt and pepper, then divide this into four patties.

6. Heat the olive oil in a pan, place the burgers in the pan and cook for around 15 minutes, flipping so both sides are browned and until any juices run clear and there is no pink or rare meat inside. Five minutes before the burgers are done, top with the cheese and cover the pan with a lid so the cheese melts.

7. Slice your buns in half, then spread ketchup on the bottom bun, place the burger on top of this, then top with tomato and lettuce.

EVERYDAY CLASSICS

Cook time
25
MINUTES

Serves
4

Chicken & Avocado Fajitas

2 tbsp olive oil
Juice of 2 limes
1 tbsp smoked paprika
1 tsp chilli powder
1 tsp ground cumin
1 tsp dried oregano
2 garlic cloves, minced
3 chicken breasts, sliced
1 onion, chopped
3 mixed peppers (I used yellow,
   orange and red), sliced
2 avocados
Handful of chopped coriander
Salt and black pepper

TO SERVE
8 wholegrain tortillas
Handful of halved cherry vine
   tomatoes
Chopped coriander
Sour cream

Chicken fajitas are such an easy and flavourful weeknight meal. Swap your usual packet mix for making fajitas for your own spice mix, without any of the unnecessary added sugar, additives and artificial flavourings.

1. Put the olive oil, 2 tablespoons of the lime juice, smoked paprika, chilli powder, ground cumin, oregano and garlic in a bowl and mix together, then add in the chicken, onion and peppers and stir to coat.

2. Transfer this to a pan and cook for 10–15 minutes until the vegetables have softened and the chicken has cooked through.

3. Mash the avocado in a bowl with 3 tablespoons of the lime juice and some salt and pepper.

4. To serve, spread the avocado on the tortillas, top with the chicken and pepper mixture and the cherry tomatoes, then sprinkle over the coriander, drizzle over the sour cream and squeeze over the rest of the lime juice.

Mozzarella & Cherry Tomato Pizza

DOUGH
300g Greek yogurt
135g self-raising flour
135g wholemeal flour
1 tsp bicarbonate of soda
½ tsp dried oregano
½ tsp garlic granules
Pinch of salt
1 tbsp olive oil

PIZZA SAUCE
200g tinned cherry tomatoes
2 tbsp tomato paste
½ tsp Italian herbs
½ tsp chilli flakes
Salt and black pepper

TOPPINGS
1–2 balls of mozzarella, sliced
Handful of cherry vine
  tomatoes, sliced
½ tsp chilli flakes
Chopped basil

This pizza recipe features a wholemeal, Greek yogurt dough that is packed with protein, making it a really satisfying meal. The pizza sauce is also simple to make yourself. I prefer using tinned cherry tomatoes for some recipes as I find them sweeter and much more flavourful.

1. Preheat the oven to 180°C.

2. Put the Greek yogurt, self-raising and wholemeal flours, bicarbonate of soda, oregano, garlic granules and salt in a bowl and mix gently until they are combined.

3. Roll the ball out into a thin circle around 1cm thick and then use your fingers to form a crust around the edge. You may need to use some flour to stop it sticking to the surface.

4. Transfer to a large baking tray, drizzle with the olive oil and bake for 10–12 minutes.

5. Meanwhile, blend the sauce ingredients together until smooth.

6. Remove the pizza from the oven and top with your sauce, the mozzarella, cherry tomatoes, some salt and pepper and the chilli flakes, then place back in the oven to bake for 5–10 minutes until the cheese is melted and the pizza is golden.

7. Serve topped with fresh chopped basil.

Cook time

1HR **30**MIN

Serves

4

Sweet Potato & Quinoa Burgers

500g sweet potatoes, chopped
2 tbsp olive oil, plus extra for
   cooking the burgers
1 red onion, finely chopped
2 garlic cloves, finely chopped
400g tin of cannellini beans
125g cooked quinoa
Juice of 1 lime
1 tsp ground cumin
1 tsp smoked paprika
1 egg
4 tbsp plain flour
2 tbsp polenta
Salt and black pepper

ROLLS AND TOPPINGS

4 wholemeal or sourdough
   buns
1 beef tomato, sliced
1 gem lettuce, sliced
6 tbsp hummus (see page 160)

Most plant-based meat replacements are unfortunately ultra-processed, so I wanted to include a vegetarian burger option that is just as delicious, so no one feels like they are missing out at a BBQ. I used cannellini beans in this recipe but feel free to swap them for other types of beans.

1. Preheat the oven to 180°C.

2. Steam the sweet potatoes for 15 minutes before mashing and then leaving to cool.

3. Meanwhile, heat the oil in a pan and cook the onion for around 5 minutes, then add the garlic and cook for 2 more minutes.

4. Partially mash the cannellini beans then mix in the quinoa, lime juice, cumin, smoked paprika, egg, flour, sweet potatoes, onion and salt and pepper.

5. Shape into four burger patties, then sprinkle polenta on each side of the burgers.

6. Pour some olive oil into a pan and cook the burgers for 3 minutes on each side until golden then bake in the oven for around 15–20 minutes until fully cooked through.

7. Slice your buns in half and place a burger patty on top, then layer up with a tomato slice and some lettuce, spreading on some hummus to finish.

Baked Squash Mac & Cheese

1 butternut squash, peeled and
  cut into chunks
4 tbsp extra virgin olive oil
1 garlic clove, minced
2 tbsp chopped sage
2 tbsp thyme leaves
60g plain flour
900ml semi-skimmed milk
2 tsp Dijon mustard
75g mature Cheddar cheese,
  grated
50g vegetarian Italian hard
  cheese, grated
400g wholegrain macaroni
Salt and black pepper

TOPPINGS
4 tbsp breadcrumbs
Grated Cheddar cheese
Thyme

This healthy twist on mac and cheese includes a serving of butternut squash, which makes the sauce super creamy. The wholegrain macaroni also adds in some extra fibre.

1. Preheat the oven to 180°C.

2. Place the butternut squash in a baking tray along with half the olive oil and some salt and pepper. Roast the squash for 20–30 minutes until soft and golden brown.

3. Cook the remaining olive oil, garlic, sage and thyme in a pan for a couple of minutes until fragrant.

4. Then add the flour and mix together. Cook this for a couple of minutes. Gradually add the milk, a bit at a time, mixing in between to avoid lumps until it thickens.

5. Stir in the mustard, cheeses and roasted butternut squash and cook for a couple of minutes, then blend until smooth.

6. Meanwhile, cook the pasta according to the package directions.

7. Stir the cooked pasta and sauce together, then transfer to an ovenproof dish and top with breadcrumbs, grated Cheddar cheese and thyme. Then grill for a few minutes until the cheese is melted and golden.

EVERYDAY CLASSICS

Crispy Prawn Tacos

with Avocado & Mango Salsa

80g plain flour
1/2 tsp powdered cayenne
 pepper
330g raw king prawns
1 egg, beaten
120g panko breadcrumbs

AVOCADO & MANGO SALSA
1 avocado, chopped into cubes
½ mango, chopped into cubes
Handful of chopped coriander
Juice of 1 lime

TOPPINGS
Sour cream
Juice of 1 lime
6–8 soft corn tortillas
Chopped coriander

Tacos are one of my favourite quick options to make for lunch or dinner. You can find non-UPF corn tortillas in some larger supermarkets or online or try making your own tacos using masa harina flour!

1. Mix the flour with the cayenne pepper. Coat the prawns in the flour mixture, then the egg, then the breadcrumbs.

2. Add a bit of oil to a pan and cook the prawns for a couple of minutes on each side until they are golden, crispy and cooked through.

3. Prepare the salsa by mixing together the avocado, mango, coriander and lime juice.

4. Mix together the sour cream and lime juice.

5. To serve, heat your corn tortillas in a pan for around a minute, then top with the avocado and mango salsa, the prawns, sour cream and some fresh chopped coriander.

Cook time

1HR.**30**MIN

Serves

4

Meatball Toad in the Hole

with Red Onion Gravy

RED ONION GRAVY

1 tbsp olive oil
3 red onions, sliced
2 tbsp plain flour
½ tsp Worcestershire sauce
1 tsp dried thyme
1 tsp Dijon mustard
500ml beef stock

BATTER

4 eggs
200ml milk
150g plain flour
4 tbsp oil (I used olive but
    sunflower or any neutral oil
    would work)
Salt and black pepper

PORK MEATBALLS

400g pork mince
2 tbsp chopped sage
1 garlic clove, chopped
2 shallots, chopped
50g breadcrumbs

TO SERVE

1 tbsp thyme leaves (optional)

This is my version of a toad in the hole using pork meatballs. I have also included a recipe for red onion gravy, so there is no need for instant gravy. This is surprisingly easy to make as it is only caramelising the onions, which is the time-consuming part!

1. To make the gravy, put the olive oil and onions in a pan and cook over a low heat for around 1 hour. Be careful not to burn the onions, so keep checking on them until they are caramelised.

2. Add the plain flour and stir to coat the onions, then add in the rest of the gravy ingredients. Turn the heat up and bring to a simmer for 10 minutes, stirring it occassionally.

3. Preheat the oven to 200°C.

4. Meanwhile, mix the eggs, milk and flour together until smooth. Season with a bit of salt and pepper and set aside.

5. Mix the meatball ingredients together and form into balls.

6. Put the olive oil and meatballs in a tin and place in the oven for 5–10 minutes to cook the meatballs and heat up the oil.

7. Add the batter to the meatballs and oil while the pan is still hot and then return to the oven for 25–30 minutes until it has risen and turned golden.

Cook time

1HR **25**MIN

Serves

4

Katsu Chicken Curry

1 egg
4 chicken breasts
50g plain flour
100g panko breadcrumbs
200g jasmine rice
200g Tenderstem broccoli

KATSU CURRY SAUCE
1 tbsp coconut oil
1 onion, chopped
1 thumb-sized piece of fresh
   ginger, grated
3 garlic cloves, minced
2 carrots, sliced
1 heaped tbsp curry powder
½ tsp ground turmeric
2 tbsp plain flour
600ml chicken stock
1 tbsp honey
1 tbsp soy sauce

TO SERVE
Chopped coriander
Chopped spring onion

Katsu curry is a restaurant and takeaway favourite, and the sauce is pretty simple to make yourself. If you want to make a vegetarian version, you can swap the chicken for tofu and reduce the cooking time slightly.

1. Preheat the oven to 200°C.

2. Put the coconut oil in a pan and cook the onion for around 5 minutes to soften. Add in the ginger, garlic and carrot and cook for a couple more minutes. Add in the curry powder, turmeric and flour and stir to coat the onions and carrots.

3. Now stir in chicken stock, honey and soy sauce. Let this simmer for 15–20 minutes until the carrots are soft and then blend until smooth.

4. Crack an egg into a bowl and beat. Dip the chicken breasts in the flour, then the egg and breadcrumbs, then place on a baking tray.

5. Bake the chicken for 25 minutes until the coating is golden and the chicken is cooked through.

6. Meanwhile, cook the rice according to the package directions and steam the broccoli for around 5–6 minutes until soft.

7. Leave the chicken to cool for around 5 minutes, then slice. To serve, place the cooked rice in a bowl, then top with the cooked chicken, the sauce and the broccoli.

Weekday
Favourites

This is a selection of some of my favourite meals to make throughout the week to give you some inspiration. It is difficult to stick to reducing UPFs in your diet with busy schedules and work or school commitments. Many of these recipes can be made in under 1 hour or prepped and frozen or kept in the fridge for super-quick meals.

Ginger, Soy & Sesame Tofu Stir-Fry

450g block of firm tofu, chopped into cubes
2 tbsp soy sauce
2 tbsp cornflour
1 tbsp coconut oil
1 red pepper, sliced
200g baby corn
200g Tenderstem broccoli
120g mangetout

SAUCE
4 tbsp soy sauce
1 tbsp grated fresh ginger
1 tbsp minced garlic
1 tbsp sesame seeds
2 tsp sesame oil
1 red chilli, finely diced
2 tbsp honey
1 tbsp cornflour
2 tbsp water

TO SERVE
Sesame seeds
Sliced red chilli
Sliced spring onion

A stir-fry is my go-to quick and easy meal and is a great way to add in lots of veggies to a meal. I like to make my own sauce rather than buying a supermarket one as these can often be ultra-processed and high in sugar.

1. Make the sauce by mixing the soy sauce, ginger, garlic, sesame seeds, sesame oil, red chilli, honey, cornflour and water together until smooth.

2. Place the tofu in a bowl, then mix with the soy sauce and cornflour.

3. Cook the tofu in a pan with a bit of oil until crispy, then set aside.

4. Add the red pepper, baby corn, Tenderstem broccoli and mangetout to the pan and cook for around 5–10 minutes until the veggies are starting to soften.

5. Add the sauce and the tofu back into the pan.

6. Once it is cooked, top with sesame seeds, chilli and spring onion to serve.

Cook time

40

MINUTES

Serves

4

Salmon Coconut Thai-inspired Curry

THAI RED CURRY PASTE
3 red chillies, deseeded
1 tsp galangal or fresh ginger
1 lemongrass stalk, sliced
4 lime leaves, sliced
2 tsp sliced coriander stalks
4 garlic cloves
4 shallots, quartered
1 tsp ground coriander
1 tsp ground cumin
1 tsp fish sauce
½ tsp salt

CURRY
1 tbsp coconut oil
4 salmon fillets
1 tsp paprika
200g shallots, chopped
2 garlic cloves, minced
1 thumb-sized piece of fresh
    ginger, grated
400ml tin of coconut milk
1 large courgette, chopped
175g baby corn, chopped
200g mangetout, chopped
Juice of 1 lime
Salt and black pepper

TO SERVE
Handful of chopped coriander
Sliced red chilli

This Thai-inspired curry is so creamy and comforting. The salmon makes a nice variation on prawns or chicken, which are typically used in this recipe. Salmon is great to include in your diet as it is rich in omega-3 fatty acids, a great source of protein and contains other nutrients, such as B vitamins, selenium and potassium.

1. Blend the curry paste ingredients into a thick paste and set aside.

2. Season the salmon fillets with salt, pepper and paprika. Heat the coconut oil in a pan and cook the salmon fillets for a couple of minutes on each side, then remove from the pan and set aside.

3. Put the shallots in the pan and cook for around 5 minutes to soften. Add in the garlic and ginger and continue cooking for a couple more minutes.

4. Pour in the coconut milk and around 4 heaped tablespoons of the curry paste. You can add more if you want it spicier.

5. Add in the courgette, baby corn and mangetout, then let this simmer for around 5 minutes.

6. Add the salmon back into the pan and let it simmer for around 5–10 more minutes.

7. Once the salmon is cooked, squeeze over the juice of 1 lime and sprinkle coriander and chilli slices.

WEEKDAY FAVOURITES

Cook time

40

MINUTES

Serves

4

Mediterranean Vegetable Halloumi Traybake

2 courgettes, chopped
1 yellow pepper, chopped
1 red pepper, chopped
1 orange pepper, chopped
1 red onion, chopped
1 tsp chilli flakes
1 tsp dried oregano
1 tsp dried basil
2 garlic cloves, minced
2 tbsp olive oil
250g cherry vine tomatoes
250g block of halloumi, sliced
Salt and black pepper

TO SERVE
Chopped basil

I love making traybakes for easy midweek meals as you only need one pan and they are so easy to throw together. I would serve this with some roasted baby potatoes, pasta or rice. This traybake is full of colour and contains two of your five a day.

1. Preheat the oven to 200°C.

2. Put the courgette, peppers and red onion, tomatoes and halloumi on a baking tray and sprinkle over the chilli flakes, dried oregano, dried basil and garlic. Drizzle over the olive oil and season with salt and pepper, then mix to evenly coat.

3. Bake in the oven for 25–30 minutes until the vegetables are soft.

4. To serve, sprinkle over fresh basil.

Red Lentil & Coconut Dal

200g red lentils
1 tbsp olive oil or coconut oil
1 onion, chopped
1 thumb-sized piece of fresh
  ginger, minced
2 garlic cloves, minced
½ tsp chilli flakes
1 tsp ground cumin
1 tsp ground coriander
1 tsp ground turmeric
1 tsp garam masala
500ml vegetable stock
400g tin of chopped tomatoes
250g coconut cream
Juice of ½ lime
Salt and black pepper

TO SERVE
Chopped coriander
400g cooked rice

This is one of my favourite plant-based recipes. The addition of coconut milk makes the dal extra creamy and delicious, which goes so well with all the spices! This recipe also freezes really well if you want to make it for meal prepping.

1. Rinse the lentils in cold water until the water is clear.

2. Heat a bit of oil in a pan, add in the onion and cook for a couple of minutes.

3. Add in ginger and garlic and continue cooking for a couple more minutes.

4. Add in all the spices and toast for a minute or two until fragrant. Pour in the stock and add the chopped tomatoes, lentils and coconut cream and season with salt and pepper.

5. Simmer for around 25 minutes, stirring every few minutes until the lentils are cooked.

6. Squeeze over the lime juice and sprinkle over coriander and then serve with rice.

Chilli Honey Halloumi Flatbread

CHILLI HONEY HALLOUMI
2 tbsp honey
Juice of ½ lemon
1 tbsp olive oil, plus extra for
frying
2 tsp chilli flakes
1 tsp chopped thyme
250g block of halloumi, sliced

TO SERVE
4 flatbreads
Tzatziki (see page 162)
Rocket
Cherry vine tomatoes,
quartered
Chopped cucumber
Chopped parsley
Pomegranate seeds

My chilli honey halloumi recipe is by far the most popular on my Instagram page, so I thought I would include it with some flatbread for an easy lunch or dinner recipe! I think the combination of the chilli flakes, honey and halloumi goes so well together.

1. First mix the honey, lemon juice, olive oil, chilli flakes and thyme together.

2. Coat the slices of halloumi in the mixture.

3. Heat a bit of olive oil in a pan, then add the halloumi and pour over any excess of the honey mixture.

4. Cook for a few minutes on each side until all the liquid has evaporated and the halloumi slices are golden and crispy.

5. To assemble, toast the flatbreads, then spread with the tzatziki and top with rocket, the halloumi, cherry tomatoes, cucumber, parsley and pomegranate seeds.

Cook time

25

MINUTES

Serves

4

Honey Garlic Prawn Noodle Stir-fry

200g wholewheat noodles
1 tbsp coconut oil
200g Tenderstem broccoli
150g baby pak choi
1 red pepper, chopped
300g cooked prawns
4 tbsp soy sauce
2 tbsp honey
1 tsp sesame oil
2 garlic cloves, minced

TO SERVE
Handful of chopped coriander
Chopped red chilli
Chopped spring onion

A noodle stir-fry is the perfect option for a midweek meal as the noodles cook so quickly while the vegetables are cooking so it comes together easily. I have made my own simple stir-fry sauce for this: honey, soy sauce, garlic and sesame oil.

1. Cook the noodles according to the package directions.

2. Meanwhile, pour the oil into a pan and add the broccoli, baby pak choi and red pepper and cook this for 5–10 minutes until they start to soften.

3. Once the noodles are done, drain them and add them to the stir-fry along with the cooked prawns, soy sauce, honey, sesame oil and garlic. Cook for a further 5 minutes while stirring to bring everything together.

4. To serve, top with the chopped coriander, red chilli and some spring onion.

V

Cook time

50
MINUTES

Serves
4

Sweet Potato, Chickpea & Aubergine Tagine

4 sweet potatoes, chopped
2 tbsp olive oil
1 large onion, chopped
2 garlic cloves, minced
2 red peppers, chopped
2 small aubergines, chopped
1 tsp ground cumin
1 tsp ground coriander
1 tsp ground cinnamon
3 tbsp harissa paste
75g dried apricots, chopped
1 tbsp honey
400g tin of chopped tomatoes
400g tin of chickpeas, drained and rinsed
300ml vegetable stock
Salt and black pepper

TO SERVE
Handful of chopped parsley
Couscous

This Moroccan-inspired, plant-based tagine is the perfect thing to cook on a rainy day because all the spices make such a warming and comforting dish. I really love the addition of the dried apricots in this as they add in a bit of sweetness.

1. Preheat the oven to 200°C.

2. Peel the sweet potato and chop into bite-sized chunks, then drizzle over half the olive oil and sprinkle over a little salt and pepper. Bake for 20-25 minutes, until soft and browned.

3. Heat a little bit of oil in a pan, fry the chopped onion for 5 minutes until soft and then add in the garlic and cook for a few minutes more.

4. Add the red pepper and cook for a few more minutes.

5. Mix in the chopped aubergine, cumin, coriander, cinnamon, harissa paste, dried apricots and honey and cook for a couple more minutes until fragrant.

6. Stir in the rest of the ingredients and simmer for 25–30 minutes until the aubergine is soft and the sauce has slightly thickened.

7. Once it's done, serve topped with chopped parsley alongside some couscous.

Cook time

1

HOUR

Serves

4

Courgette & Pea Risotto

1 tbsp olive oil
300g shallots, finely chopped
2 courgettes, chopped
2 garlic cloves, finely chopped
300g arborio rice
1–1.5 litres vegetable stock
200g frozen petits pois
30g vegetarian Italian hard
    cheese, grated, reserving
    some for the top
Juice and zest of 1 lemon
Salt and black pepper

TO SERVE
Chopped parsley
Toasted pine nuts

I love making risotto and changing up the ingredients depending on the season. I used shallots in this one, which I love trying in place of onions sometimes as they are much milder and add in a lot of flavour.

1. Gently toast the pine nuts in a dry frying pan for 1 minute, and set aside.

2. Heat a bit of olive oil in a pan, add the shallots and cook for a few minutes until soft.

3. Add in the courgettes, garlic, then cook for a couple more minutes.

4. Add in the arborio rice and stir to coat in the shallots and oil.

5. Pour in the stock around 1/4 cup at a time, stirring over a low heat for 25–30 minutes until the rice is nearly cooked.

6. Ten minutes before the end of cooking, add in the peas, cheese, lemon juice and zest.

7. Serve topped with chopped parsley and the toasted pine nuts.

Cook time

25

MINUTES

Serves

2

Prawn Poke Bowl

180g sushi rice
150g prawns
1 tsp honey
2 tbsp soy sauce
¼ cucumber, cubed
½ mango, cubed
½ avocado, cubed
Handful of radishes, sliced
2 tbsp Greek yogurt
1 tsp chilli garlic sauce (see tip)

TO SERVE
1 tbsp sesame seeds
2 spring onions, trimmed and
    chopped

Poke bowls are one of my favourite quick things to get when eating out, so I thought I could include a simpler one to make at home using prawns rather than raw fish! Once all the vegetables are chopped for this recipe, it is so simple and quick to put together.

1. Cook the sushi rice according to the package directions and divide into two bowls.

2. Meanwhile, coat the prawns in the honey and soy sauce and then cook in a pan for a couple of minutes until the prawns are fully cooked through.

3. Top the bowls with the cucumber, prawns, mango, avocado and radishes.

4. Mix together the Greek yogurt and chilli garlic sauce and drizzle this over, then sprinkle over sesame seeds and spring onion to serve.

TIP
A lot of sauces found in supermarkets can be ultra-processed but not all of them are. When choosing the sauces for your recipes, try and opt for something with minimal ingredients that you recognise and would use in your own kitchen, with no additives or flavour enhancers.

Cook time

40

MINUTES

Serves

4

Cajun Prawn Pasta

1 tbsp olive oil
1 red onion, diced
2 red peppers, diced
400g cherry vine tomatoes
2 garlic cloves, crushed
2 tbsp Cajun seasoning
1 tsp chilli flakes, plus extra
   for the top
2 tsp smoked paprika
4 tbsp tomato paste
200g cream cheese
100–200ml vegetable or
   chicken stock
400g pasta (I used brown rice
   fusilli)
Handful of Parmesan cheese,
   plus extra for the top
300g cooked king prawns
Juice of 1 lemon

TO SERVE
Chopped parsley

Most dried pasta you can find in supermarkets is non-ultra-processed as it only contains one or two ingredients. Yes, even white pasta! If you want to increase the fibre and protein in your pasta dishes, you can also swap for a wholegrain variety, lentil pasta or brown rice pasta.

1. In a pan, heat the oil, add in the onion and cook for a few minutes until soft.

2. Add in the red pepper, cherry tomatoes and garlic and continue to cook for a further 5 minutes.

3. Add in the Cajun seasoning, chilli flakes, smoked paprika, tomato paste, cream cheese and 100ml stock and simmer for around 20 minutes or until everything is soft and well combined. You can add more stock if the sauce is too thick.

4. Meanwhile, cook the pasta according to the package directions.

5. Once the sauce is done, stir in the Parmesan, king prawns and pasta and cook for a few more minutes. Add a bit of pasta water if the sauce is too thick.

6. Squeeze over the lemon juice and sprinkle over the parsley, chilli flakes and Parmesan to serve.

VG

Cook time
30
MINUTES

Serves
4

Leek, Spinach & Butter Bean Stew

1 tbsp olive oil
2 shallots, diced
2 leeks, washed, trimmed and sliced
2 garlic cloves, finely chopped
1 tbsp plain flour
300ml vegetable stock
2 x 400g tins of butter beans
Juice and zest of 1 lemon
4 large handfuls of spinach, chopped
2 tbsp chopped chives, plus extra to serve
2 tbsp chopped parsley, plus extra to serve
8 slices of sourdough bread
Salt and black pepper

Dishes using beans have become so popular on social media recently and for good reason! Using tinned beans allows you to make a really filling and satisfying meal that is also high in fibre quickly and easily.

1. Put the olive oil in a pan along with the shallots and leeks and cook for around 5–10 minutes, stirring every little while until the leeks are soft.

2. Add in the garlic and cook for a couple more minutes.

3. Then add in the flour and stir to coat everything.

4. Pour in the vegetable stock, add the butter beans and allow this to simmer for around 10–15 minutes until thickened slightly.

5. Stir in the lemon juice and zest, the spinach, chives and parsley and allow the spinach to wilt for a couple of minutes, stirring to combine.

6. To serve, top with more chives and parsley and serve with some sourdough bread.

VG

Cook time
30
MINUTES

Serves
4

Sticky Cashew Tofu

CRISPY TOFU
450g block of firm tofu, chopped into cubes
4 tbsp cornflour
½ tsp garlic powder
½ tsp Chinese five-spice
2 tbsp olive oil
Salt and black pepper

SAUCE
100g cashews
6 spring onions, trimmed and chopped
1 tbsp olive oil
1 red pepper, chopped
1 orange pepper, chopped
1 thumb-sized piece of fresh ginger, grated
2 garlic cloves, minced
1 tbsp cornflour
6 tbsp soy sauce
3 tbsp rice vinegar
3 tbsp chilli garlic sauce
2 tsp sesame oil

TO SERVE
Chopped spring onion
Sesame seeds
400g cooked rice
200g Tenderstem broccoli

This sticky cashew tofu is like having a takeaway meal but made at home. Tofu is an ingredient a lot of people think of as being bland or boring, but it doesn't have to be! It is all about adding a really flavourful sauce and making sure to season your tofu before cooking.

1. Gently toast the cashews in a dry frying pan for 1 minute.

2. Coat the tofu in the cornflour, garlic powder, Chinese five-spice and salt and pepper.

3. Add oil to the pan and fry the tofu for a few minutes until it's crispy, turning the pieces every little while so all the sides are cooked.

4. Remove from the pan and set aside, then in the same pan cook the spring onion in the oil until soft. Add in the red and orange peppers and cook for a few more minutes.

5. Add in the ginger, garlic, cornflour, soy sauce, rice vinegar, chilli garlic sauce and sesame oil and cook for a few more minutes until the sauce has thickened slightly.

6. Add in the tofu and cashews and stir into the sauce. Cook this for a few minutes until the sauce is coating the tofu.

7. Top with spring onion and sesame seeds and serve with rice and steamed Tenderstem broccoli.

Cook time

1HR **20**MIN

Serves

4

Meatball Casserole

1 tbsp olive oil
1 onion, chopped
2 garlic cloves, minced
5 celery sticks, chopped
2 carrots, grated
1 yellow pepper, chopped
1 red pepper, chopped
2 tsp smoked paprika
1 tsp ground cumin
1 tsp dried thyme
2 x 400g tins of cherry
   tomatoes
500ml vegetable stock
400g tin of cannellini
   beans, drained and rinsed

MEATBALLS
400g beef mince
1 egg
50g breadcrumbs
2 tbsp chopped coriander
2 garlic cloves, minced
Salt and black pepper

TO SERVE
Chopped parsley

This is my twist on a sausage casserole using beef meatballs in place of the sausages. The sauce is packed with lots of different veggies and some cannellini beans to add more texture and flavour.

1. Heat a bit of oil in a pan and fry the onion for 5 minutes then add the garlic, celery, grated carrot, yellow and red pepper.

2. Continue cooking for 5–10 minutes until the vegetables start to soften.

3. Meanwhile, in a bowl mix together meatball ingredients and roll into even-sized ball and then in another non-stick pan cook the meatballs for around 5–10 minutes until they are browned on the outside, then set aside.

4. To the pan with the onion, add in the smoked paprika, cumin and thyme and cook for a couple more minutes until it becomes fragrant.

5. Mix in the cherry tomatoes, stock and cannellini beans and let the sauce simmer for around 15 minutes.

6. Now add in the meatballs and continue cooking for a further 20–25 minutes.

7. Season with salt and pepper and sprinkle over fresh parsley to serve.

Sides, Salads & Dips

This chapter has the perfect dip and side additions to your weeknight meals, alongside some delicious salads for lighter and more summery meals that are so fresh and colourful. I have also included a couple of savoury snack ideas as it can be difficult to find non-UPF options for these.

Watermelon, Feta, Mint & Basil Salad

1 watermelon, cubed
1 cucumber, chopped
2 tbsp honey
2 tbsp olive oil
Juice of 1 lime
2 tbsp honey
1 tsp chilli flakes
Handful of chopped mint leaves, reserving some for the top
Handful of chopped basil leaves, reserving some for the top
100g feta, crumbled
Salt and black pepper

Watermelon salads are one of my favourite things to make in the summer. They are so refreshing and I really love the combination of fruit and cheese together. I think this is the perfect thing to make as a side for a summer BBQ as it is so easy to throw together!

1. To a bowl add the watermelon, cucumber, honey, olive oil, lime juice, chilli flakes, mint leaves, basil leaves, salt and pepper, then gently mix this together.

2. Move to a serving bowl and top with crumbled feta cheese and some more chopped mint, basil and a sprinkle of salt and pepper.

Cook time

1
HOUR

Serves

4–6
AS A SIDE

Herby Potato Salad

750g baby potatoes, halved
4–6 tbsp Greek yogurt
Juice of 1 lemon
Bunch of spring onions,
 trimmed and chopped
2 tbsp chopped chives, plus
 extra for the top
Handful of chopped dill
4 tbsp capers
Salt and black pepper

I always forget how much I love potato salad until I make it. For this version I have swapped mayo for Greek yogurt as most supermarket mayo is UPF and this is an easier swap than making your own mayo. It also decreased the fat and increased the protein in the salad slightly!

1. Heat a pan of water and boil the baby potatoes for around 20 minutes until soft and then drain and leave to cool down.

2. Once cooled down, add in the Greek yogurt, lemon, spring onions, chives, dill and capers and season with salt and pepper.

3. Mix to combine and then sprinkle over some extra chives to serve!

Cook time
30
MINUTES

Serves
4

Chicken Caesar Salad
with Chickpea Croutons

CHICKPEA CROUTONS
400g tin of chickpeas, drained and rinsed
1 tbsp olive oil
2 tsp garlic granules
½ tsp dried oregano
1 tsp dried parsley
Salt and black pepper

DRESSING
6 tbsp Greek yogurt
Juice of 1 lemon
30g Parmesan cheese, grated
1 tbsp white wine vinegar
Dash of Worcestershire sauce
1 garlic clove, minced
2 anchovies

SALAD
400g baby leaf mixed green salad
2 avocados, chopped
4 cooked chicken breasts, shredded
Grated Parmesan

I love swapping romaine or iceberg lettuce in salads with something much more nutrient-dense, like mixed baby leaves or even kale, and this also gives salads like this much more flavour! I also swapped the traditional croutons here for some delicious garlic-roasted chickpeas.

1. Preheat the oven to 200°C.

2. Put the chickpeas in a bowl along with the olive oil, garlic granules, oregano, parsley and salt and pepper and mix to coat the chickpeas.

3. Spread the chickpeas in a thin layer on a baking tray and bake for around 20 minutes until they are golden and crispy, then set aside.

4. In a food processor, blend the Greek yogurt, lemon juice, Parmesan cheese, white wine vinegar, Worcestershire sauce, garlic and anchovies to form a smooth and creamy dressing.

5. To assemble the salad, start with a bed of the baby leaves, avocado and shredded chicken and then sprinkle over the chickpea croutons and Parmesan and drizzle over the dressing to serve.

V

Cook time
15
MINUTES

Serves
6–8
AS A SIDE

Healthier Coleslaw

100g Greek yogurt
1 tbsp Dijon mustard
1 tbsp white wine vinegar
½ small white cabbage, chopped
½ small red cabbage, chopped
4 carrots, grated
1 large red onion, chopped
3 tbsp chopped dill, plus extra for the top
3 tbsp chopped parsley, plus extra for the top
3 tbsp chopped chives, plus extra for the top
Salt and pepper, to taste

This homemade coleslaw tastes so much fresher than shop-bought versions and is the perfect slaw to serve at a BBQ or in sandwiches. I have even used this recipe in fresh corn tortillas alongside grilled salmon to make tacos.

1. In a large bowl, mix together the Greek yogurt, Dijon mustard and white wine vinegar to combine.

2. Add the white cabbage, red cabbage, carrot, red onion, dill, parsley, chives, salt and pepper and mix to coat the coleslaw evenly.

3. Serve topped with more of the dill, parsley and chives.

Cook time
10
MINUTES

Serves
2

Strawberry, Balsamic & Avocado Salad

120g mixed green salad (I used a baby green lettuce, spinach, baby red lettuce, chard mix)
100g strawberries, chopped
100g cherry vine tomatoes, halved
½ avocado, chopped
125g mozzarella cherries, drained
Salt and black pepper
Balsamic glaze

I love adding fruit to a salad and the strawberries and balsamic glaze work so well together! This salad would be great for a BBQ or as a lunch or dinner with some added protein such as grilled chicken or fish.

1. Put the mixed green salad in a large serving bowl, then top with the strawberries, cherry tomatoes, avocado and mozzarella cherries.

2. Sprinkle over salt and pepper and drizzle over the balsamic glaze.

Roasted Corn Salad

8 small corn cobs or 4 large
3 tbsp olive oil
Juice and zest of 1 lime
1 garlic clove, finely grated
1 red pepper, chopped
1 avocado, finely chopped
200g cherry vine tomatoes, halved
1 cucumber, diced
2 spring onions, thinly sliced
1 red chilli, finely chopped
Handful of chopped coriander, plus extra for the top
Salt and black pepper

This corn salad is the perfect salad to make in the summer or for a BBQ if you are looking for something a bit different than your average salad. The zesty dressing goes so well with all the crunchy fresh vegetables and the creamy avocado.

1. Preheat the oven to 200°C.

2. Place the corn in a roasting tin and drizzle over the olive oil and salt and pepper. Roast in the oven for around 15 minutes until the corn starts to turn golden.

3. Leave the corn to cool down, then cut the kernels off the cobs and place in a mixing bowl.

4. Add the lime juice and zest, garlic, red pepper, avocado, cherry tomatoes, cucumber, spring onion, chilli and a handful of coriander. Season with salt and pepper.

5. Mix this all together, then transfer to a serving bowl and top with some more chopped coriander.

Cook time

40
MINUTES

Serves
2–3 AS MAIN
4 AS A SIDE

Sweet Potato, Halloumi & Za'atar Salad

700g sweet potatoes, peeled and chopped
400g tin of chickpeas, drained and rinsed
3 tbsp olive oil
1 tbsp za'atar, plus 1 tsp extra to serve
250g block of halloumi, sliced
200g mixed green salad (I used a pea shoots, baby spinach, baby chard mix)
Pomegranate seeds

DRESSING
3 tbsp lemon juice
3 tbsp olive oil
1 tsp maple syrup
Pinch of salt and black pepper

This is a twist on one of my most popular Instagram recipes, using sweet potatoes instead of squash. Salads can make such a great option for lunch to get in lots of veggies! This salad can be made for meal prep – just make sure to keep all the parts separate until you want to eat it, so nothing gets soggy.

1. Preheat the oven to 200°C.

2. Put the sweet potato and chickpeas on a baking tray, drizzle with a bit of olive oil and sprinkle over the za'atar.

3. Roast the chickpeas and sweet potato for around 20–25 minutes until the potato is soft and golden.

4. Meanwhile, make your dressing by combining the lemon juice, olive oil, maple syrup and salt and pepper in a bowl.

5. In a pan with a bit of oil, cook the halloumi until golden brown.

6. To assemble the salad, mix the sweet potato and chickpeas into the mixed green salad.

7. Top with the cooked halloumi and pomegranate seeds, and you can sprinkle with more za'atar. Drizzle over the dressing to serve.

Cook time
30
MINUTES

Makes
6
FLATBREADS

No-knead Garlic Flatbreads

300g Greek yogurt
135g self-raising flour
135g wholemeal flour
1 tsp bicarbonate of soda
Pinch of salt
2 tbsp olive oil
2 garlic cloves, minced

TO SERVE
Chopped parsley

This is the easiest and quickest way I have found to make bread at home. There is no need to spend hours waiting for the bread to rise or kneading it! The base of the bread only requires five ingredients and you can change the oil or seasoning for it depending on what you want to pair it with!

1. Put the Greek yogurt, self-raising and wholemeal flours, bicarbonate of soda and salt in a bowl and mix gently until they are combined. You may need to switch to your hands to get the flour fully mixed in.

2. Tip onto a work surface and bring together into a smooth ball with your hands.

3. Divide the ball into six even-sized pieces and roll a piece into a thin oval shape.

4. Heat a non-stick pan with around 1 tablespoon of the olive oil and place the rolled-out dough into the pan.

5. Cook for a couple of minutes on each side until golden brown and it rises slightly, then place onto a plate to cool down. Continue with the rest of the flatbreads.

6. Mix the remaining olive oil with the garlic cloves and brush onto the finished flatbreads.

7. Sprinkle over chopped fresh parsley to serve.

Cook time

1
HOUR

Serves
4

Garlic & Parmesan Squashed Potatoes

750g baby potatoes
3 tbsp olive oil
2 garlic cloves, minced
25g Parmesan cheese, grated
Salt and black pepper

TO SERVE
Chopped parsley

These potatoes have been really popular on social media, and they make such a delicious side dish for a weeknight dinner that is a bit different to your normal roasted or mashed potato. You could also try adding some chilli flakes, chilli powder or smoked paprika for a spicier version.

1. Heat a pan of water and boil the baby potatoes for around 20 minutes until soft and then drain and leave to cool down.

2. Meanwhile, mix together the olive oil, garlic and Parmesan, season with salt and pepper and then set aside.

3. Preheat the oven to 200°C and line a baking tray with baking paper.

4. Place the potatoes on the baking tray evenly spaced out. You may need to use two to three baking trays so the potatoes are spread out.

5. Use a potato masher to crush the potatoes and then drizzle over the Parmesan and olive oil mixture.

6. Bake in the oven for around 30 minutes until crispy and golden.

7. To serve, sprinkle over parsley.

VG

Cook time

1

HOUR

Makes

24

CRACKERS

Poppy Seed & Sesame Crackers

275g oats
2 tbsp poppy seeds
2 tbsp sesame seeds
50ml olive oil
100ml boiling water
Salt and black pepper

Making your own crackers may seem daunting but is surprisingly easy. I really love using oats in place of flour in some of my recipes as they are high in fibre, including a beneficial type of fibre called beta-glucan, and provide micronutrients such as zinc, copper, selenium and B vitamins.

1. Preheat the oven to 200°C and line a baking tray with baking paper.

2. Gently toast the sesame seeds in a dry frying pan for 1 minute.

3. Put the oats in a food processor and blend to form a flour. Add the flour to a bowl with the poppy seeds, sesame seeds, olive oil and boiling water and season with salt and pepper. Mix this to form a dough – you may need to use your hands.

4. Place the dough ball between two sheets of baking paper and roll out until it's 5mm thick using a rolling pin. Cut out circles and place these on the prepared baking tray. Re-roll the dough and repeat until you have used it all.

5. Bake the crackers for 20 minutes until golden brown.

6. Leave them to cool down before serving or you can store them in an airtight container for a few days.

7. I served mine here topped with hummus, cherry tomatoes and cress.

VG

Cook time
10
MINUTES

Makes
6–8
PORTIONS

Quick & Easy Hummus

2 x 400g tins of chickpeas,
   drained and rinsed
4 tbsp olive oil
2 garlic cloves, minced
Juice and zest of 1 lemon
80g tahini
Pinch of sea salt flakes

TOPPINGS
Olive oil
Chickpeas
Handful of coriander
Chilli flakes

Hummus is such an easy dip to make at home and a great snack paired with some veggies or bread. I have used this hummus recipe in a few of the other recipes as well if you are looking for other ways to use it.

1. Put all the ingredients in a food processor and blend until smooth.

2. Place the hummus in a bowl, then drizzle over olive oil and sprinkle over the chickpeas, coriander and chilli flakes.

Cook time
10
MINUTES

Serves
4–6
AS A SIDE

Lemon & Dill Tzatziki

½ cucumber, grated
200g Greek yogurt
Juice of ½ lemon
1 garlic clove, minced
2 tbsp chopped dill, plus extra
for the top
2 tbsp chopped parsley, plus
extra for the top
1 tbsp olive oil, plus extra for
the top
Salt and black pepper

Tzatziki is one of my favourite dips to make in the summer as it is so refreshing! I love making it with dill but another variation of this recipe would be to use mint, which would go really nicely with a spicy dish.

1. First squeeze the grated cucumber in a clean tea towel to remove excess liquid.

2. Add to a bowl along with the Greek yogurt, lemon juice, garlic, dill, parsley and olive oil, then season with salt and pepper.

3. Mix together until combined and then finish with more olive oil, dill and parsley.

4. I serve mine with some toasted pitta.

VG

Cook time
30
MINUTES

Serves
4–6
AS A SIDE

Black Bean Salsa
with Tortilla Chips

SALSA
400g tin of black beans,
   drained and rinsed
285g tin of sweetcorn, drained
150g cherry vine tomatoes,
   chopped
1 red onion, chopped
1 red or green chilli, chopped
1 garlic clove, minced
Large handful of chopped
   coriander
Juice of 1 lime
1 tablespoon olive oil
1 tsp ground cumin
Salt and black pepper

TORTILLA CHIPS
4 wholegrain tortillas (see tip)
1 tsp olive oil

This bean salsa is full of protein and I have paired it with homemade wholegrain baked tortilla chips to dip into it. They make a great alternative to shop-bought tortilla chips as they aren't fried, so contain much less fat!

1. Preheat the oven to 180°C.

2. Put the black beans, sweetcorn, cherry tomatoes, red onion, chilli, garlic, coriander, lime juice, olive oil and cumin in a bowl and season with salt and pepper.

3. Mix this together and then set aside.

4. Meanwhile, slice your tortillas into triangles and spread onto a couple of baking trays, then drizzle with olive oil.

5. Bake the tortilla chips for 8–10 minutes, flipping halfway through.

6. Serve the salsa with the tortilla chips.

TIP
When choosing your tortillas, try and opt for something with minimal ingredients and additives.

Something Sweet

Desserts and sweet treats can still be enjoyed in moderation when trying to eat a healthier diet with less UPFs. Most homemade desserts are not ultra-processed, but if you are also looking to reduce the sugar in your diet, I have included some healthier twists on classic dessert and baking recipes!

Five-ingredient Chocolate Oat Biscuits

200g oats
175g almond butter
60ml maple syrup
½ tsp bicarbonate of soda
100g dark chocolate

These biscuits are so simple to make and perfect with a cup of tea or coffee. They only require five ingredients to make, most of which you probably already have at home! I dipped mine in dark chocolate, but they will be equally as delicious without it.

1. Preheat the oven to 170°C. Line a baking tray with baking paper.

2. Put the rolled oats in a food processor and pulse a few times to form a coarse flour.

3. Add the oats to a mixing bowl along with the almond butter, maple syrup and bicarbonate of soda and mix to form a dough.

4. Press around 1 to 2 tablespoons of the dough into a biscuit cutter to make an even round shape and place on the prepared baking tray. Repeat with the remaining dough.

5. Bake the cookies for 12–13 minutes until golden brown, then let them cool completely.

6. Once cool, melt the dark chocolate in a heatproof bowl set over, but not touching, a pan of simmering water, and half dip the cookies.

7. Leave the chocolate to fully set before eating.

SOMETHING SWEET

Cook time
15
MINUTES

Makes
2
MOUSSES

Avocado Chocolate Mousse

50g dark chocolate
2 large avocados
55g cocoa powder
3 tbsp maple syrup
Pinch of sea salt

TO SERVE
2 heaped tbsp Greek yogurt
Strawberries
2 tbsp chocolate chips or chopped or grated dark chocolate

Using avocado gives this mousse a rich, creamy texture without using any dairy or eggs. It can be made quickly using a food processor to create a really healthy vegan mousse. Avocados are packed with healthy fats and are a great source of a lot of different nutrients.

1. Melt the dark chocolate in a heatproof bowl set over, but not touching, a pan of simmering water.

2. Put the melted chocolate, avocado, cocoa powder, maple syrup and sea salt in a food processor and blend until smooth.

3. Once the mousse is smooth, spoon the mousse into serving glasses and then top with Greek yogurt and fresh strawberries.

4. Finally, top with chocolate chips or chopped or grated dark chocolate to serve.

Cook time

1
HOUR

Makes
8–10
PORTIONS

Orange, Polenta & Pistachio Cake

250g unsalted butter, softened, plus extra to grease the tin
250g golden caster sugar
4 eggs
Juice and zest of 2 large oranges
200g ground almonds
150g polenta
2 tsp baking powder
30g pistachios, chopped
1 tbsp icing sugar

Polenta isn't just for savoury recipes and can be so delicious when used in baking. It gives this cake a really dense and moist texture and I think it goes really well with the orange and pistachio flavour.

1. Gently toast the pistachios in a dry frying pan for 1 minute, and set aside.

2. Preheat the oven to 180°C and grease and line a 23cm springform tin.

3. Use an electric whisk to beat the butter and sugar until pale and fluffy.

4. Add in the eggs, along with the orange juice and zest, and beat again until combined.

5. Add in the ground almonds, polenta and baking powder and fold this in.

6. Place in the springform tin and bake for around 40–45 minutes until golden, risen and a toothpick comes out clean when inserted in the middle.

7. Leave the cake to cool fully before removing from the tin.

8. To serve, top with the pistachios and icing sugar.

Cook time

1
HOUR

Serves
6

Apple & Berry Crumble

CRUMBLE
75g ground almonds
150g oats
80g butter
60g sugar, plus 2 tbsp for
    the fruit
400g frozen mixed summer
    berries
1–2 apples, cubed
Juice and zest of 1 orange

VANILLA CUSTARD
1 vanilla pod
500ml milk
3 egg yolks
2 tbsp caster sugar
1 tbsp cornflour

I love making crumble with an oaty topping because I think it goes so well with fruit and custard! I've included a custard recipe to go along with the crumble, but you could also serve it with some cream if you prefer!

1. Preheat the oven to 170°C.

2. Put the ground almonds, oats, butter and 60g sugar in a bowl and rub together until the butter is fully combined.

3. Put the fruit and remaining sugar in a baking dish.

4. Place the crumble topping evenly on top of the fruit and bake in the oven for around 50 minutes–1 hour.

5. Meanwhile, make the custard by scraping the vanilla seeds out of the pod and putting them both in a pan along with the milk. Bring to a boil, then remove the vanilla pod.

6. In a bowl, whisk together the egg yolks, sugar and cornflour and then gradually add the milk. Be careful as you don't want to cook the egg.

7. Pour the mixture back into the pan and cook gently over a low heat for around 20 minutes until thickened. Make sure to whisk it every little while so there are no lumps.

8. Serve the crumble topped with the custard.

SOMETHING SWEET

Cook time

45

MINUTES

Makes

9

BROWNIES

Peanut Butter Swirl Brownies

200g dark chocolate

200g butter

1 tsp vanilla extract

3 eggs

200g golden caster sugar

150g ground almonds

4 tbsp natural peanut butter, melted

I used melted dark chocolate in these brownies to make them really indulgent and delicious. Ground almonds were also used in place of flour to help create a moist and fudgy texture, which is perfect for brownies and makes them naturally gluten-free.

1. Preheat the oven to 180°C and line a 23cm square baking tin.

2. In a heatproof bowl set over, but not touching, a pan of simmering water, gently melt the chocolate and butter.

3. To the same bowl add the vanilla extract, eggs, caster sugar and ground almonds and mix to combine.

4. Pour the batter into the prepared baking tin. Melt the peanut butter, then drizzle this over the batter. Use a butter knife to marble this in.

5. Bake for 25–30 minutes until the brownie is set and cooked through, then leave to cool down fully.

6. Cut into nine slices to serve.

Pumpkin Seed & Raisin Oat Bars

100g butter
100g honey
250g oats
1 egg
50g pumpkin seeds
80g raisins, chopped
½ tsp ground cinnamon
Pinch of salt

If you are looking for an easy snack you can take to school or work, try making these oat bars. I have used an egg here to help bind together the ingredients so not as much butter and honey are required. An egg or egg white can also be used to make slightly healthier crumble toppings or granola.

1. Preheat the oven to 180°C and line a 23cm square baking tin with baking paper.

2. Melt the butter and honey together in a pan over a low heat, stirring every little while.

3. Take off the heat and stir in the oats, egg, pumpkin seeds, raisins, cinnamon and a pinch of salt.

4. Spoon the mixture into the prepared tin and press until it is flattened.

5. Bake for around 20 minutes until golden brown, then leave to cool down fully before slicing.

6. You can store in an airtight container for a few days.

VG

Cook time
15
MINUTES

Makes
20
BALLS

Chocolate Hemp Seed Protein Balls

200g Medjool dates
150g shelled hemp seeds
150g ground almonds
3 tbsp almond butter
4 tbsp cocoa powder

TO COAT
30g shelled hemp seeds

It can be difficult to find high-protein snacks when trying to reduce UPFs in your diet, especially something sweet! If you have specific protein needs or just want a really satisfying snack, then these are the perfect thing to make. These contain 11g protein per two balls.

1. Put the Medjool dates, hemp seeds, ground almonds, almond butter and cocoa powder in food processer and blend together until a smooth paste is formed.

2. Roll the paste into 20 even-sized balls. You may need to put the paste in the fridge for a bit if it is too sticky to roll.

3. Roll half of the balls in hemp seeds.

4. The balls can be stored in the fridge in an airtight container for a few days.

VG

Cook time
10
MINUTES

Serves
4

Popcorn
3 Ways

CLASSIC
1 tbsp coconut oil
120g popcorn kernels
Pinch of salt

CINNAMON
1 tsp ground cinnamon

MATCHA DARK CHOCOLATE
2 tsp matcha powder
50g dark chocolate

Making your own popcorn at home is such an easy non-UPF snack! I have included three examples of flavours here, but you can change it up depending on what you already have at home.

1. Heat a little bit of oil in a pan and add one popcorn kernel.

2. Put the lid back on and let it pop. Once it pops, it's hot enough to add the rest.

3. Add the rest of the kernels and heat over a low heat while they pop. Once there are around 5 seconds between pops, turn off the heat and leave to cool with the lid on.

4. You can simply sprinkle over a little bit of salt to serve or alternatively add some more toppings.

For the cinnamon
For this flavour, sprinkle over cinnamon and then stir or shake the popcorn to fully coat.

For the matcha dark chocolate
1. For this flavour, sprinkle over the matcha and then stir or shake the popcorn to fully coat.

2. In a heatproof bowl set over, but not touching, a pan of simmering water, gently melt the chocolate.

3. Drizzle the melted dark chocolate over the popcorn.

SOMETHING SWEET

Meal plan *for 4 people*

I have put together an example meal plan and shopping list using the recipes in this book to help give you some ideas on how you use these recipes at home.

	BREAKFAST	LUNCH	DINNER	SNACK/DESSERT
MONDAY	Berry Compote Porridge	Spiced Baked Beans on Toast	Roasted Tomato Gnocchi	Orange, Polenta & Pistachio Cake
TUESDAY	Sourdough French Toast	Leek, Asparagus & Pea Frittata	Smoky Stuffed Peppers	Orange, Polenta & Pistachio Cake
WEDNESDAY	Chocolate Peanut Butter Banana Porridge	Creamy Tomato Soup	Chicken & Avocado Fajitas	Five-ingredient Chocolate Oat Biscuits
THURSDAY	Meal Prep Breakfast Sandwich	Chickpea Curry Jacket Potatoes	Classic Spaghetti Bolognese	Five-ingredient Chocolate Oat Biscuits
FRIDAY	Healthier Cooked Breakfast	Carrot, Coconut & Lentil Soup	Roasted Mediterranean Vegetable Lasagne	Chocolate Hemp Seed Protein Balls
SATURDAY	Oat & Greek Yogurt Pancakes	Three Bean Chilli Soup	Crispy Prawn Tacos	Cinnamon & Classic Popcorn
SUNDAY	Berry Breakfast Muffins	Avocado & Tomato Tuna Melts	Traybake Roast Chicken	Apple & Berry Crumble

Conversion tables

WEIGHT

Metric	Imperial
15g	½ oz
25g	1 oz
100g	4 oz
150g	5 oz
275g	10 oz
350g	12 oz
400g	14 oz
425g	15 oz
450g	1 lb
900g	2 lb
1.5kg	3 lb

VOLUME

Metric	Imperial
25ml	1 fl oz
50ml	2 fl oz
150ml	5 fl oz (¼ pint)
300ml	10 fl oz (½ pint)
450ml	15 fl oz (¾ pint)
900ml	32 fl oz
1 litre	1¾ pints
1.5 litres	2½ pints

Metric	Cups
60 ml	quarter cup
80 ml	third cup
120 ml	half cup
240 ml	cup

OVEN TEMPERATURES

°C	°F
150°C	300°F
160°C	325°F
180°C	350°F
190°C	375°F
200°C	400°F
220°C	425°F
230°C	450°F

References

1. Rauber F, da Costa Louzada ML, Martinez Steele E, de Rezende LFM, Millett C, Monteiro CA, et al. 'Ultra-processed foods and excessive free sugar intake in the UK: A nationally representative cross-sectional study'. *BMJ Open*. 2019 Oct; 9(10).

2. Elizabeth L, Machado P, Zinöcker M, Baker P, Lawrence M. 'Ultra-processed foods and health outcomes: A narrative review'. *Nutrients*. 2020 Jun 30;12(7):1955.

3. Lane MM, Gamage E, Du S, Ashtree DN, McGuinness AJ, Gauci S, et al. 'Ultra-processed food exposure and adverse health outcomes: Umbrella review of epidemiological meta-analyses'. *BMJ*. 2024 Feb 28.

4. Whelan K, Bancil AS, Lindsay JO, Chassaing B. 'Ultra-processed foods and food additives in gut health and disease'. *Nature Reviews Gastroenterology & Hepatology*. 2024 Feb 22.

5. Cordova R, Viallon V, Fontvieille E, Peruchet-Noray L, Jansana A, Wagner K-H, et al. 'Consumption of ultra-processed foods and risk of multimorbidity of cancer and cardiometabolic diseases: A multinational cohort study'. *The Lancet Regional Health - Europe*. 2023 Dec; 35:100771.

6. Martini D, Godos J, Bonaccio M, Vitaglione P, Grosso G. 'Ultra-processed foods and nutritional dietary profile: A meta-analysis of nationally representative samples'. *Nutrients*. 2021 Sept 27;13(10):3390.

7. Monteiro CA, Cannon G, Lawrence M, da Costa Louzada ML and Pereira Machado P. 2019. 'Ultra-processed foods, diet quality, and health using the NOVA classification system'. Rome, FAO.

Index

INDEX

Acknowledgements

First and foremost, I would like to thank my followers for supporting me and making this possible. I'm so grateful I get to share my passion for food and nutrition with so many people. I hope this book serves as a helpful tool for eating a healthier diet and less ultra processed foods.

I would like to thank my dad for his unwavering support through weeks of recipe testing, tight deadlines and being my most enthusiastic taste tester. His invaluable feedback and creative recipe ideas were essential in creating each recipe.

I would also like to express my gratitude to my publisher, Ebury, for believing in this project and providing the resources and support needed to make it a reality. To my editor, Sam thank you for your meticulous attention to detail and for ensuring that every recipe is clear and accessible.

1

Pop Press, an imprint of Ebury Publishing
Penguin Random House UK
One Embassy Gardens, 8 Viaduct Gdns,
Nine Elms, London SW11 7BW

Pop Press is part of the Penguin Random House group of companies
whose addresses can be found at global.penguinrandomhouse.com

Penguin
Random House
UK

Text copyright © Delicia Bale 2024
Photography by Delicia Bale

Delicia Bale has asserted her right to be identified as the author of this
Work in accordance with the Copyright, Designs and Patents Act 1988

No part of this book may be used or reproduced in any manner for the purpose of training artificial
intelligence technologies or systems. In accordance with Article 4(3) of the DSM Directive 2019/790,
Penguin Random House expressly reserves this work from the text and data mining exception.

First published by Pop Press in 2024

www.penguin.co.uk

A CIP catalogue record for this book is available from the British Library

ISBN 9781529941708

Printed and bound in Italy by L.E.G.O. S.p.A.

The authorised representative in the EEA is Penguin Random House Ireland,
Morrison Chambers, 32 Nassau Street, Dublin D02 YH68.

MIX
Paper | Supporting
responsible forestry
FSC® C018179
www.fsc.org

Penguin Random House is committed to a sustainable
future for our business, our readers and our planet.
This book is made from Forest Stewardship Council®
certified paper.